Wetlands of Tanzania

IUCN—The World Conservation Union

Founded in 1948, IUCN – The World Conservation Union brings together States, government agencies and a diverse range of non-governmental organizations in a unique world partnership: some 650 members in all, spread across 120 countries.

As a union, IUCN exists to serve its members—to represent their views on the world stage and to provide them with the concepts, strategies and technical support they need to achieve their goals. Through its six Commissions, IUCN draws together over 5000 expert volunteers in project teams and action groups. A central secretariat coordinates the IUCN Programme and leads initiatives on the conservation and sustainable use of the world's biological diversity and the management of habitats and natural resources, as well as providing a range of services. The Union has helped many countries to prepare National Conservation Strategies, and demonstrates the application of its knowledge through the field projects it supervises. Operations are increasingly decentralized and are carried forward by an expanding network of regional and country offices, located principally in developing countries.

IUCN – The World Conservation Union seeks above all to work with its members to achieve development that is sustainable and that provides a lasting improvement in the quality of life for people all over the world.

IUCN Wetlands Programme

The IUCN Wetlands Programme coordinates and reinforces activities of the Union concerned with the management of wetland ecosystems. The Programme focuses upon the conservation of ecological and hydrological processes, in particular by developing, testing, and promoting means of sustainable utilisation of wetlands. It does so in collaboration with IUCN members and partners, in particular those other international institutions with a specific wetland mandate, especially the Ramsar Convention Bureau, and the International Waterfowl and Wetlands Research Bureau (IWRB).

The core of the Programme is a series of field projects which develop the methodologies for wetland management, in particular in the countries of the developing world where wetlands are used intensively by local communities which depend upon these for their well-being. Related strategic and policy initiatives draw upon the results of these projects and present their conclusions in a form useful for government decision makers and planners.

The activities of the Programme are designed on the basis of the concerns and information provided by IUCN members. To facilitate this, the Programme works through IUCN's regional offices. The Programme also works closely with the major development assistance agencies to ensure that conservation considerations are adequately addressed in their projects.

The Wetlands Programme receives generous financial support from the World Wide Fund For Nature (WWF), the Swiss Directorate of Development Cooperation and Humanitarian Aid (DDA), the Finnish International Development Agency (FINNIDA) and the Government of the Netherlands. Project support has been received from the Swedish International Development Authority (SIDA), Norwegian Agency for Development Cooperation (NORAD), United States Agency for International Development (USAID), the Ford Foundation and a number of IUCN members including the Finnish Association for Nature Conservation (FANC), Institut Français pour le Développement en Coopération (ORSTOM), the Royal Society for the Protection of Birds (RSPB), the United States National Park Service (USNPS) and the World Wide Fund For Nature (WWF). It is coordinated from the IUCN Headquarters in Switzerland, with regional coordinators in Central America, South America, Brazil, West Africa, southern Africa and Asia.

Wetlands of Tanzania

Proceedings of a Seminar on the Wetlands of Tanzania,
Morogoro, Tanzania, 27-29 November, 1991

Editors

G.L. Kamukala and S.A. Crafter

IUCN
1993

Published by: IUCN

IUCN
The World Conservation Union

Citation: Kamukala, G.L. and Crafter, S.A. (Eds), 1993. *Wetlands of Tanzania.*
Proceedings of a Seminar on the Wetlands of Tanzania, Morogoro,
Tanzania, 27-29 November, 1991. vi + 170 pp.

ISBN: 2-8317-0185-6

Designed and typeset: Samara Publishing Ltd, Tresaith, Dyfed, SA43 2JG, UK

Cover design: Sarah Skinner

Cover photograph: Lower Rufiji Floodplain. G.W. Howard

Available from: IUCN Communications Division, Rue Mauverney 28,
1196 Gland, Switzerland

Contents

Introduction

G.W. Howard

Regional Wetlands Programme
IUCN Regional Office for Eastern Africa
P.O. Box 68200
Nairobi
Kenya

The United Republic of Tanzania is a large country situated on the eastern side of southern and central Africa. The mainland area has 20 Regions (Figure 1), each containing at least four districts. Offshore in the Indian Ocean, Zanzibar consists of the main island (Unguja) together with several smaller islands and Pemba Island, while Mafia Island is part of the Coast Region. Tanzania has eight neighbouring countries (Figure 1) and is part of both the Southern African Development Community (formerly SADCC) and the Preferential Trade Area of eastern and southern Africa (PTA).

Tanzania has a diverse morphology which includes the highest and largest mountain in Africa (Kilimanjaro, 5,895 m), the deepest lake in Africa (Tanganyika, maximum depth 1,470 m), the largest lake in Africa (Victoria, entire area in three countries of around 70,000 km^2) and river systems that flow into the Indian Ocean, the Atlantic Ocean and the Mediterranean Sea (Figure 2). The eastern and western arms of the Rift Valley are also present within Tanzania which results in spectacular scenery, endorheic drainage basins and many different types of wetlands (Figures 2 and 3). Several medium sized lakes and two large impoundments (Figure 2) contribute lacustrine wetlands while the river systems (Figure 2) produce flood plains and other associated riverine wetlands. The distribution of the major wetlands is shown in Figure 3 which has a similar scale to Figures 1 and 2 for location of these wetlands in relation to regions, rivers and lakes.

A comparison of the three Figures also shows that there is a lake, a river or a large wetland on each of Tanzania's borders with its neighbouring countries. Specifically, Tanzania shares Lakes Chala, Jipe and Natron with Kenya; Lake Victoria with Kenya and Uganda; the Kagera River swamps and floodplains with Uganda and the middle Kagera swamps and lakes with Rwanda. Tanzania and Burundi have the Malagarasi River and its tributary on their common boundary, while Tanzania shares Lake Tanganyika with Burundi, Zaire and Zambia, and Lake Nyasa with Malawi and Mozambique. The Ruvuma River runs along most of the common land border with Mozambique. Thus there are major wetlands and lakes requiring trans-boundary management and cooperation all around Tanzania, with

Figure 1   Map of Tanzania showing the regions and the positions of neighbouring countries

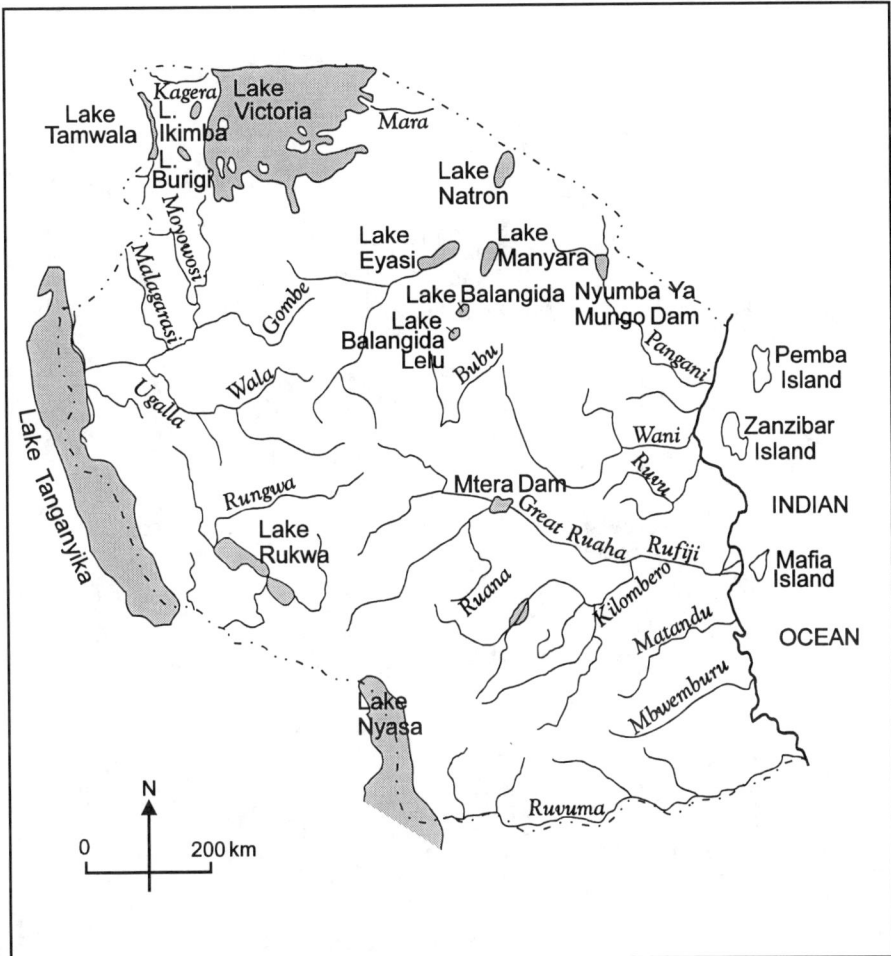

Figure 2   Map of Tanzania showing river systems, lakes and major dams

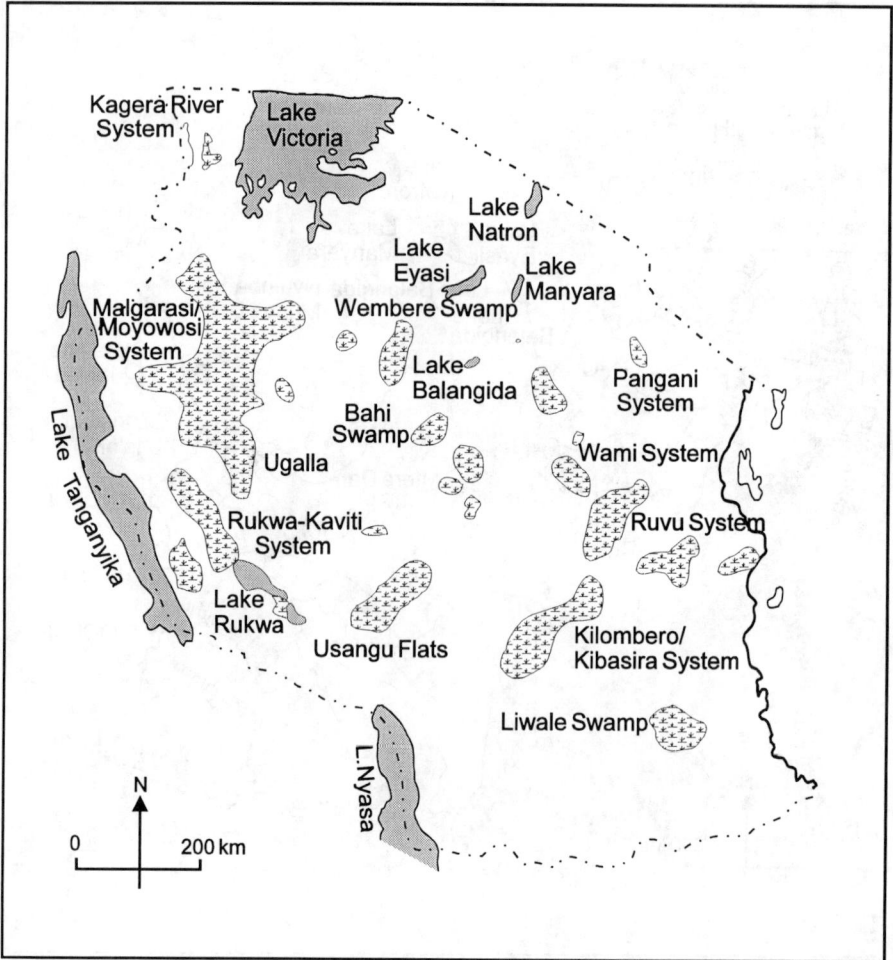

Figure 3   Major wetlands of Tanzania

marine wetlands on the seaward side which are part of a coastal system shared (in an ecological sense) with Kenya, Mozambique and the Indian Ocean states.

The term 'wetland' is used in this volume to describe ecosystems that are based upon water and which fit with the Ramsar definition as detailed in its Article 1, namely:

> "areas of marsh, fen, peatland or water, whether natural or artificial, permanent or temporary, with water that is static or flowing, brackish or salt, including areas of marine water the depth of which does not exceed six metres".

This definition has been used here because it groups together ecosystems that may have common needs for management as well as common ecological pathways and mechanisms. Many types of Tanzanian wetlands are described in the following contributions to the Seminar, but all are combinations of water, light and air with influences from soils, and all have wetland vegetation resulting from these components. It is this vegetation which characterises different types of wetlands and, in turn, determines the fauna and human uses in many cases. By bringing together considerations of these comparable water-based ecosystems, it is possible to examine the different sectoral perspectives for their use and thus develop strategies for multisectoral appreciation and management of wetlands.

Tanzania's numerous and varied national (and international) wetland resources are beginning to be threatened by overutilisation and inadequately planned management as well as by a lack of basic information and public awareness of their values, functions and products. These developing threats to wetlands could be lessened by a national programme of conservation and wise use of wetland resources and by interaction with neighbouring countries with similar resources and problems.

The development of a wetland conservation and management programme for Tanzania was the subject of a cooperative investigation by WWF, IUCN and the National Environment Management Council (NEMC) of the Ministry of Tourism, Natural Resources and Environment in March 1990. This resulted in a comprehensive report (NEMC/WWF/IUCN, 1990) which listed the wetland resources of Tanzania and proposed a number of models for a national wetlands programme. The report and its conclusions were then considered by government in early 1991 and it was decided that Tanzania should develop a national programme. In June of 1991 Tanzania attended the SADCC Wetlands Conservation Conference (Matiza and Chabwela, 1992) and participated in the recommendation of that meeting that each SADCC country should formulate its own wetlands programme. Subsequent discussions among the institutions involved led to the proposal to hold a National Seminar on the Wetlands of Tanzania to examine the issues and to develop proposals for the structure of a national wetlands programme. This meeting was also designed to raise awareness of government officers and the public about the importance of Tanzania's wetlands and the need for their wise use. The Seminar was planned so that its proceedings and findings could be published in a form that could offer guidance to future wetlands programme operatives and, at the same time, assemble contemporary information and development options for the nation's wetlands.

The Seminar was organised by NEMC with assistance from the IUCN Regional Office for Eastern Africa. Funding was provided by the Headquarters and Wetlands Programme of IUCN which receives support from the Finnish International Development Agency (FINNIDA). The meeting was held at the Morogoro Hotel from 27th to 29th November, 1991, and was attended by participants, contributors and visitors who all assisted with the development of the Seminar Resolutions (published in this volume).

Bibliography

NEMC/WWF/IUCN. 1990. *Development of a wetland conservation and management programme for Tanzania.* IUCN, Gland, Switzerland. 113 pp.

Matiza, T. and H.N. Chabwela. (Eds). 1992. *Wetlands Conservation Conference for Southern Africa. Proceedings of the SADCC Wetlands Conference held in Gaborone, Botswana, 3-5 June, 1991.* IUCN, Gland, Switzerland. 224 pp.

Opening address to the Seminar on Wetlands of Tanzania

Delivered by E.K. Mugurusi on behalf of Mr P. Mkanga, Principal Secretary, Ministry of Tourism, Natural Resources and Environment

It is indeed a privilege and great pleasure for me to officiate at the opening of this very important Seminar on the Wetlands of Tanzania.

On behalf of the Government of the United Republic of Tanzania and on my own behalf, I extend a warm welcome to you all and hope you will enjoy your time in Morogoro. I am informed that this forum brings together academics, researchers, policy makers, environmentalists, and people with vast experience in wetland conservation from both within and outside Tanzania.

I am especially indebted to resource people from Kenya, Uganda and Zambia for their efforts to join us during this seminar. It is my conviction that with such wide scope and expertise you will be able to discuss the theme exhaustively. I am therefore confident that the seminar will make practical and effective recommendations.

I am also informed that the presentations will cover a wide range of aspects concerning wetlands, including: geomorphology and origin of wetlands; resources of wetlands in broad perspective; wetland functions, products and attributes; and issues governing the rational utilisation of wetlands. Drawing from experiences of our friendly and brotherly countries of Kenya, Uganda and Zambia, you will be able to contribute a great deal not only towards academic satisfaction but also towards a comprehensive National Conservation Strategy for Tanzania, which is under preparation.

A seminar on the status, utilisation and conservation of wetlands is an important activity at a time when environmental issues are at the top of the agenda worldwide. Although wetlands in Tanzania contribute significantly to the socio-economic status of our people, there has never been such a gathering to bring to light the role which these endowments play in the nation.

Lake margins, rivers, swamps, marshes, floodplains, peatlands, mangrove forests, coastlines and dams all possess more or less similar characteristics. These characteristics make them valuable to man and precious habitats for a wide range of animals and plants.

Wetlands in Tanzania are regarded by some as pockets of land accommodating water and vegetation. To others, they are regarded as sources of fish, places to cultivate rice, areas to provide water for livestock, or sources of papyrus for rafts, mats or baskets. Whatever the perception, wetlands are potential areas of social and economic importance. They are sources of energy, are capable of being harnessed for irrigation in large scale farming and are important in livestock husbandry.

However, interventions are necessary to protect wetlands against degradation. In Tanzania, a number of development projects have been undertaken on or near wetlands, without regard to environmental degradation and pollution. Often, environmental impact assessment (EIA) does not precede project implementation. It is imperative that EIAs become an integral part of project preparation and appraisal in all development endeavours. This is relevant for environmental integrity in general and wetland conservation in particular. Protection of the environment, of which wetlands constitute an important part, is vital for sustainable development. Wetlands support various animals and plants, some of which are endemic.

The maintenance of the ecological balance in wetlands is essential and their utilisation must be properly managed. However, also of importance are the priorities of the Tanzanian people who depend on wetland resources. Balance between opposing needs will only be achieved if the following areas are given consideration: conservation of fragile and endemic ecosystems; adoption of measures for rational utilisation of wetlands and related areas; protection of watersheds, especially upper catchment areas; maintenance of forests; protection of biodiversity; prevention of land degradation and restoration of damaged lands; and careful allocation and management of the wetland resource base.

Moreover, since the perceived needs for wetlands conservation and utilisation cut across a wide range of issues, I recommend that you consider the following: adoption of cross-sectoral planning and management; proposals for broader and coordinated systems at the national, regional and district levels; increased environmental education, public awareness and involvement; and need for coordinated regional utilisation of wetlands.

Conservation of wetlands is not the same as protection and it should be viewed as a positive move embracing restoration, enhancement, and rational utilisation for the attainment of sustainable development. No country can achieve sustainable development without a sound natural resource base. Our wetlands need our consolidated efforts, commitment and involvement for their sustainability.

May I once again express my appreciation and pleasure that this important seminar is attended by notable experts in the field of wetlands. This representation is a sign of commitment and interest in this field. I am grateful to the World Conservation Union (IUCN) for sponsoring this seminar.

I wish this seminar all the success and at this juncture I have the honour to declare it OPEN.

An overview and scope of Tanzanian wetlands

G.L. Kamukala

Director General
National Environment Management Council
P.O. Box 63134
Dar es Salaam

Introduction

Tanzania is very rich in wetland resources which include the Great Lake systems, major river networks and deltaic mangroves. The major lakes and floodplains have long provided a fertile resource base as they include alluvial plains of great agricultural potential.

Wetlands in Tanzania support an extensive trading and transport system, fishing grounds, agro-pastoral activities, hydrological processes and, more recently, the harnessing of the river flows for irrigation and hydroelectric power.

As wetland systems are developed, multiple values inherent in these systems are either ignored or underestimated during their planning in favour of a single interest or sector. With hindsight, there is increasing awareness not only of the free benefits accruing from intact wetland systems but also of the social, environmental and socio-economic costs of disruption of those systems. Degradation and loss of natural systems can increase the already intense pressures on rural communities.

Well managed, these productive ecosystems can help meet the needs of a rising population with increased demands and can alleviate environmental problems.

Overview of Tanzania's wetlands

General outline

Tanzania is the largest country in East Africa and she enjoys a significant proportion of the wetlands. The Indian Ocean coast is 1,000 km long with a highly indented coastline. In the southwest, there is a shoreline of 305 km on Lake Nyasa and another of 650 km on Lake Tanganyika in the west. To the northwest, 1,420 km of Lake Victoria's shoreline lies in Tanzania (NEMC/WWF/IUCN, 1990).

9

Tanzania is drained by a number of rivers and streams. Because of the general declination from the western and central highlands towards the coast, much of the country drains to the ocean. A few large rivers drain away from the coast, for example, the Kagera and Mara Rivers drain into Lake Victoria and the Malagarasi River drains into Lake Tanganyika. Swampy basins and floodplain wetlands are common in Tanzania; estimates indicate that almost 10% of the country's surface area is covered by wetlands (NEMC/WWF/IUCN, 1990).

The principal wetland systems are: the Western and Eastern Rift Valley lakes, Lake Victoria, numerous minor lakes, riverine floodplains and permanent swamps, coastal mangrove systems with intertidal mudflats, and a number of artificial impoundments constructed for hydropower and irrigation.

Approximately 2.7 million hectares are covered by areas of permanent or seasonal freshwater swamps and seasonal floodplains, distributed over almost all of the country's major river systems. Another striking feature is the mangrove forests which support a richly varied environment and occur along the Tanzanian coast from the Kenyan border in the north to the Mozambique border in the south.

Wetland values and functions

Research and surveys have provided empirical evidence to show that wetlands are among the most productive ecosystems of Tanzania (Loma, 1979; LRDC and ODA, 1987; Bwathondi and Ngoile, 1990; Mwalyosi, 1990; Semesi, 1990). These fabulous natural resources are continually being depleted and only rarely is sustainable utilisation considered. Wetlands are multifunctional with diverse values and functions. They include agricultural, hydrological, ecological, logistical and social values.

Fisheries

It is estimated that over 110,000 artisanal fishermen are engaged in the fishing industry (DANIDA, 1989). The fishery potential in the large lakes is not known, while fish biomass in Tanzanian coastal waters is 100,000-200,000 t. Swamps, rivers and reservoirs play a very important role in total fish supply because of their wide distribution throughout the country. Mangroves, estuaries, deltas and shallow offshore waters are vital for maintaining coastal finfish, shrimp and mollusc fisheries.

Agriculture

In many floodplain areas rice has been grown for centuries. Maize is often grown as a flood recession crop during the dry season. Most of these crops are grown without additional fertilisers and rely on the natural fertility of wetlands and alluvial soils.

Irrigated systems seek to intensify rice production using improved varieties, mechanised techniques, improved water management and appropriate fertilisers and pesticides. Other crops, such as cotton and sorghum perform well in lowlands which have black cotton soils and silty soils respectively.

Livestock

Wetlands play an important role in the ecosystem supporting livestock herds, especially in the semi-arid grassland areas. Floodplains in the northern part of the country can support densities of 1-2 head/ha. This is because the dynamics of floodplain systems continually makes new pastures available as others dry out; cattle are thus permanently on the move and cause less damage than if they remained in one location. Extensive herding could be an excellent use of flood-plain resources during the dry season and, if adequately planned and controlled, can be completely compatible with other land uses.

Hydrology

Wetlands, when in their natural state, can play an important role in the water cycle through their numerous functions summarised below:

1. **Groundwater recharge**
   Water filters down from the wetland into an underground aquifer which stores potable water.

2. **Groundwater discharge**
   Water that has been stored underground moves out of the aquifer to become surface water.

3. **Flood control**
   By storing precipitation and releasing the water slowly, wetlands can diminish the destructive effects of flood crests downstream.

4. **Nutrient cycling**
   Wetlands can filter and recycle soil nutrients, preventing eutrophication of rivers and lakes.

5. **Micro-climate stabilisation**
   The overall hydrological, nutrient and energy cycles of wetlands may stabilise local climatic conditions, particularly rainfall and temperature. This in turn influences agricultural or resource-based activities (Dugan, 1990).

6. **Storm protection and shoreline stabilisation**
   Mangrove forests help to dissipate the force of storms and lessen damage to the ecosystem. Wetland vegetation can stabilise shorelines by reducing the energy of waves, currents, or other erosive forces.

7. **Biomass export**
   Many wetlands support dense populations of fish, cattle or wildlife which feed on the nutrient rich waters, substrates, or graze on the lush pastures.

8. **Sediment retention**
   Although it is upland areas which suffer soil loss, it is the downstream system which has to cope with high sediment loads. In 1990, torrential rains clogged otherwise fertile fields in the southern zone of Tanzania.

Wildlife resources

Many of the species which have made Tanzania renowned for its wildlife are migratory and have well-defined dry and rainy season habits which include wetlands. Many wetlands are rich in wildlife which provides important recreational and food resources and commercial products including hides, skins and trophies. Unfortunately, human activities have caused some species to become endangered while others are threatened with extinction.

Water supply

Wetlands have always been a source of water for human and livestock consumption, and to supply agriculture and industry. They are often oases in areas of low rainfall, making such places habitable.

Biological diversity

Many wetlands support spectacular concentrations of flora and fauna. For example Lakes Victoria, Tanganyika and Nyasa support over 700 species of endemic fish (NEMC/WWF/IUCN, 1990). Moreover, wetlands are important as genetic reservoirs for certain plant species, including waterlilies and wetland rice. Without proper conservation many species could be lost.

Threats to wetlands

The following activities are threats to the integrity of wetlands in Tanzania:
1. Cutting of aquatic and other vegetation for fuel, housing, commercial activities, etc.
2. Overgrazing and overcultivation by pastoralists and farmers.
3. Illegal and improper fishing practices.
4. Pollution by domestic sewage, industrial effluent, and agro-chemicals.
5. Development activities, including dam construction, coastal development, mining and quarrying.
6. Eutrophication may be caused by point 4 and leads to oxygen depletion.
7. Establishment of new human and livestock settlements.
8. Hunting and killing of wildlife.
9. Introduction, illegally or otherwise, of non-traditional or alien species into wetlands (e.g. water hyacinth, nile perch).

Major issues in wetland development

To halt or minimise degradation of wetland resources, legislation must be linked to an improved understanding of the resources and ecosystems. This entails increased public sensitisation and awareness of the benefits of wetlands. The call for cross-sectoral awareness of wetland values and functions is important. Projects need centralised or inter-ministerial coordination to ensure harmonised endeavours. Environmental assessment should be carried out for the sustained management of development projects.

People should be made to appreciate the true socio-economic, biological and scientific importance of wetlands and assisted to change from a harvesting to a management approach.

In order to change national policies, which are deficient in the promotion of wetland conservation, a policy which takes care of sustainable wetlands management is already under way. Many wetlands are lost because of faulty planning methods. Inter-sectoral planning, which involves appropriate tools and approaches, should be developed to facilitate this process.

There is not enough data on wetland ecosystems, their functions or their possible responses to different forms of development pressure. More information is needed in order to ascertain the extent of wetland development and utilisation, and to establish wetland monitoring.

Conclusion

The wetlands scattered throughout Tanzania are the product of many years of geological, hydrological and climatological processes, combined with the activities of living organisms and overlain by human land use patterns. Wetland management should take into account the dynamic nature of wetlands. Therefore, for any changes to be effective, the wise use of wetlands requires a broad view of all parties concerned.

Sectors with activities related to the utilisation of wetlands should join hands. It is thus expected that participants at this meeting will generate recommendations on how wetland conservation should become part of the national conservation effort.

Plans for the wise use of wetlands should be coordinated to include a whole basin approach (including uplands and coastal areas) for management and protection of the complex and diverse systems. The understanding of wetlands, as highly productive ecosystems with a wide range of functions which are important to people, is growing along with the recognition that losses and threats to these systems have severe consequences.

Bibliography

Burbridge, P.R. 1990. Overview of the Management of Wetland. Paper presented to the Wetland Management Workshops. IUCN General Assembly, Perth, Australia, December 1990.

Bwathondi, P.O.J. and M.A.K. Ngoile. 1990. Environmental Aspects of the Utilisation of Aquatic Resources. Paper presented at a workshop on the National Conservation Strategy, Dodoma, Tanzania, 12-17 November, 1990.

Cohen, A.S. 1989. Criteria for developing reliable underwater natural reserves in Lake Tanganyika. Paper presented at the International Symposium on Resource Use and Conservation of the African Great Lakes. Bujumbura, Burundi.

DANIDA. 1989. *Environmental profile: Tanzania*. DANIDA, Copenhagen, Denmark. 71 pp.

Dugan, P.J. (Ed.). 1990. *Wetland Conservation: A Review of Current Issues and Required Action*. IUCN, Gland, Switzerland. 96 pp.

Loma, A.J. 1979. Crop water requirements and beneficial flood for the Rufiji flood plain agriculture. Unpublished report, Institute of Resource Assessment, University of Dar es Salaam.

LRDC and ODA. 1987. Profile of Agricultural Potential in Tanzania. Land Resources Development Centre (LRDC) and Overseas Development Assistance (ODA), Surbiton, UK. Unpublished report.

Mwalyosi, R.B.B. 1990. Resources potentials of the Rufiji basin, Tanzania. *Ambio* 19(1):16-20.

NEMC/WWF/IUCN. 1990. *Development of a Wetland Conservation and Management Programme for Tanzania*. IUCN, Gland, Switzerland. 113 pp.

Ntakimazi, G. 1989. Conservation of the Resources of the African Great Lakes: Why? Paper presented to the International Symposium on Resource Use and Conservation of the African Great Lakes, Bujumbura, Burundi.

Semesi, A. 1989. Conserving the Mangrove forests of East Africa: the case of the Rufiji Delta Mangrove. Paper presented to the workshop on Marine Sciences in East Africa. 14-16 November, Dar es Salaam, Tanzania.

Semesi, A. 1990. Conservation and utilisation of mangrove plants along the Tanzania Coast. Paper presented to the National workshop on Plant Genetic Resources, Arusha, Tanzania. January, 1990.

Conservation of wetlands of Tanzania

B.L.M. Bakobi

NEMC
P.O. Box 63154
Dar es Salaam

Summary

The major wetland systems of Tanzania are described together with specific functions, products and attributes of lakes, rivers, swamps, estuaries, mangroves and coastal areas. Reasons and priorities for the conservation of wetlands are given together with the existing problems of wetland conservation and their solutions.

Introduction

Wetlands have historically been regarded as wastelands but they can also be viewed as being among the last truly wild and untouched places in the world (Maltby, 1986). In Tanzania, the productive nature of these ecosystems has not been valued and they have been threatened by development.

In the words of the former President of IUCN, we have

> "sought to exploit the riches of these habitats, we have unwittingly destroyed them. Unconscious of their fragility we have, in our attempt to increase productivity, so disturbed the natural system that productivity has declined in several places"

(Swaminathan, in Maltby, 1986).

Tanzania is endowed with exceptional wetland resources, ranging from substantial lake systems to river floodplains and deltaic mangrove formations. Most of these wetlands are seen as areas in need of development. Those which have been tapped have shifted from multi-functionality towards mono-functionality.

Wetland ecosystems have great functional diversity. When well managed, these productive habitats can satisfy many needs of the people while their degradation and loss can adversely affect both people and the endemic biota of wetland ecosystems.

'Wetland' is a collective term for ecosystems whose formation has been dominated by water, and whose processes and characteristics are largely controlled by water

(Maltby, 1986). They constitute a wide range of inland, coastal and marine habitats which share a number of common features (Dugan, 1990).

Although there are as many definitions for wetlands as there are types of groups of wetlands, the Ramsar Convention (1988) provides the broadest one, which is used in this paper (see Introduction). The Ramsar Convention defines a wide range of wetland habitat types according to their basic biological and physical characteristics. For detailed discussion, six categories (lakes, rivers, marshes and swamps, floodplains, estuaries and mangroves) have been selected from the 39 categories of wetlands identified by the Convention. Table 1 summarises the various values of these and other categories of wetlands.

This paper highlights the most important wetlands of Tanzania. In order to appreciate their importance and the need for wetland conservation, a brief description of their functions and uses follows.

The wetlands of Tanzania

Physical characteristics of the country

The total area of the Tanzanian mainland is 945,000 km^2 of which 883,500 km^2 is land, and 61,500 km^2 is covered by water (Bureau of Statistics, 1989). The country lies just south of the equator (1-12°S) and is bounded by the Great Lakes (Victoria, Tanganyika and Nyasa) on one side and the Indian Ocean on the other. The country has an equatorial and sub-equatorial climate. Rainfall ranges from 450 mm/year in the arid areas to 2,000 mm/year in the highlands and coastal belt. The average annual temperature ranges from 20-25°C with considerable variation in different regions due to the effect of altitude (LRDC and ODA, 1987).

A major distinctive feature of Tanzania's topography is the Great Rift Valley, marked by long, narrow and deep depressions often containing wetlands. Most of the major lakes in Tanzania are within the two arms of the Rift.

Tanzania has a complex drainage system; there is a general declination from the western highlands towards the highly indented coastline. The principal water-courses from the north or northwest drain the eastern margin and slopes of the interior plateau. The northwestern highlands, along the border with Rwanda and Burundi, drain either to Lake Victoria or to the endorheic Lakes Burigi and Ikimba. Further south, the mainland drains into Lake Tanganyika and the endorheic Rukwa Basin. The trough of the eastern Rift Valley drains into a series of soda lakes (Manyara, Eyasi, Natron) while the Bahi Swamp, near Dodoma, drains the surrounding areas and hills to the north. The major rivers, lakes and wetlands are shown in Figures 1 and 2 in the Introduction to this volume.

Table 1   Values of wetlands in Tanzania (Source: Dugan, 1990, with modifications)

	Value/wetland category	Lakes	Rivers	Marshes (freshwater) and swamps	Estuaries/ delta (without mangroves)	Floodplains	Mangroves	Open coasts	Man-made wetlands (reservoirs, ponds, waterways, etc.)
1.0	**Functions of wetlands**								
1.1	Groundwater recharge	++	++	+	o	++	o	o	o
1.2	Groundwater discharge	+	+	++	+	+	+	+	+
1.3	Flood control	++	+	++	++	++	++	-	o
1.4	Shoreline stabilisation, erosion control	-	++	+	+	o	++	+	-
1.5	Sediment/toxicant retention	++	o	++	+	++	++	+	+
1.6	Nutrient retention	+	o	++	+	++	++	+	+
1.7	Biomass export	+	o	+	+	++	++	+	+
1.8	Storm protection/windbreak	-	o	o	+	-	++	+	o
1.9	Micro-climate stabilisation	+	+	+	o	+	+	o	o
1.10	Navigability (water transport)	++	+	o	o	o	-	++	+
1.11	Recreation/tourism	++	++	o	+	o	+	++	+
2.0	**Wetland products**								
2.1	Fisheries (fish, crustaceans, molluscs)	++	+	+	+	o	+	++	+
2.2	Agriculture (grains, cotton, etc.)	+	+	++	+	++	-	o	+
2.3	Water supply (domestic uses, livestock, industrial)	++	++	+	+	+	-	-	++
2.4	Forest resources (charcoal, timber, etc.)	+	+	o	-	o	++	+	o
2.5	Wildlife resources	+	+	+	+	+	++	+	o
2.6	Grazing for livestock	o	o	++	++	++	+	o	o
2.7	Others (papyrus, ornaments)	++	++	++	-	+	o	-	+
3.0	**Attributes of wetlands**								
3.1	Biodiversity	++	+	++	++	++	++	++	o
3.2	Socio-cultural/heritage importance	++	++	+	+	+	++	++	-

++   Common and important   +   Present

o   May be present   -   Absent or exceptional

The major wetland systems

It is estimated that wetlands cover over 7% of the country's surface area (NEMC/WWF/IUCN, 1990). The extensive open water areas and fringing swamps of the Great Lakes cover 5.2 million ha. Tanzania owns 47% of Lake Victoria, 45% of Lake Tanganyika and 20% of Lake Nyasa (Bwathondi, 1990). The remaining permanent freshwater lakes, account for only 45,000 ha (NEMC/WWF/IUCN, 1990). On the other hand, Tanzania possesses enormous areas of permanent and seasonal freshwater swamps, marshes and seasonal floodplains, distributed over most of the country's major river systems and covering 2.7 million ha. The largest in this category is the Rufiji- Ruaha River system which has wetlands covering 695,500 ha. Other river systems are: the Malagarasi-Moyowosi system (partly in the Moyowosi Game Reserve), and the Pangani, Wami, Ugalla, Siuwe, Ruvu, Kagera and Mara Rivers.

The Little and Great Ruaha Rivers in the highlands have many small, seasonal and permanent marshes and swamps on acidic soils. At maximum flooding, Lake Rukwa and its associated fresh to brackish swamps and floodplains cover some 700,000 ha, making it one of Tanzania's largest wetland areas. The system includes Katavi plain, Kafufu Swamp, and the floodplain of the Msaginya River.

Equally important wetland systems are the alkaline waters and lakes, endorheic swamps and freshwater swamps. Lake Eyasi is a seasonal alkaline lake of 116,000 ha. However, elsewhere in the Eyasi Basin there are large floodplains at Wembere, along the Nyahura River and the permanent freshwater Lake Kitangiri (36,000 ha). In the Manyara Basin are Lake Manyara, an alkaline lake of 42,300 ha, Shuriro Swamp and floodplain system, Tarangire Swamp, and the swamps at the headwaters of the Kisaki River.

Important endorheic wetlands include the Bahi Swamp (125,000 ha), Yaida Swamp, the sodic Lake Natron (85,500 ha), Lake Burigi (a brackish lake of 7,000 ha), Lake Ikimba (12,500 ha), the alkaline lakes Balangida (6,000 ha) and Balangida Lclu (3,000 ha), Endeshi Swamp, and a number of smaller saline lakes and crater lakes, mostly in the northeast of the country.

There are over 85,000 ha of man-made wetlands in Tanzania. The most important impoundments include the Mtera Dam (61,000 ha), Lake Nyumba ya Mungu (18,000 ha) and Mindu Dam.

The coastal wetlands (200,000 ha) are covered predominantly by mangroves which are concentrated in the sheltered creeks on the mainland and offshore islands. In some of the deltas and estuaries, the mangroves form a transition between the marine environment and the freshwater swamps further inland. The Rufiji Delta has the largest stand of mangroves on the entire East African coast (Semesi, 1989), accounting for 50% of all mangroves in Tanzania (Table 2). Other important mangrove areas include Mwanza, Tanga, the mouths of the Wami, Ruvu, Matandu and Ruvuma Rivers. Islands such as Mbegani, Kunduchi, Latham, Kisiju, Kivinje, Kilwa and Mafia have appreciable mangrove forests (Semesi, 1988; Semesi, 1989).

Table 2   Mangrove forests of Tanzania (Source: Bwathondi 1990)

District/Region	Area (ha)
Muheza and Tanga	9,403
Pangani	1,755
Bagamoyo	5,636
Dar es Salaam	2,168
Kisarawe	3,858
Rufiji	53,255
Mafia	3,473
Kilwa	22,439
Lindi	4,564
Mtwara	8,942

Functions, products and attributes of wetlands in Tanzania

Worldwide, wetlands are known for their ability to support a large human population. Many authors (Odum, 1971; Simmons 1981; Maltby, 1986; Dugan 1990; Kamukala, 1990; Stuart, 1990) stress that wetlands are, and will continue to be, essential to the health, welfare and safety of people who live in or near them (Table 1). Simmons (1981) affirms that wetlands are among the most productive ecosystems and thus deserve special attention. Empirical evidence shows that some wetlands can produce up to eight times as much plant matter as an average wheat field (Maltby, 1986).

Wetlands are also important for ground water recharge, control of floods, retention of sediments, preventing eutrophication of rivers and lakes, supporting specific biota and traditional uses (Table 1). In order to conceptualise the importance of wetlands in Tanzania, the roles of the main wetland ecosystems are highlighted.

Lakes

Wetlands are often formed on lake margins, extending from the shallow littoral zone out to the deeper limnetic zone where light penetrates to support rooted vegetation (Dugan, 1990). Depending on the nature of the marginal vegetation, many lacustrine wetlands are able to intercept overland runoff and stream flow and thus influence water quality by moderating the amount of nutrients and sediment that enter the lake (Kurata and Kira, 1990; Pieczynska, 1990).

Freshwater fisheries contribute 80% of the fish production in Tanzania (Bwathondi, 1990). Common species in the lake shores, muddy bays and surround- ing marshy areas include *Protopterus aethiopicus* (lungfish, 'Kamongo'), *Clarias mossambicus* (catfish, 'Mumi' or 'Kambale'), and species of *Tilapia*, *Oreochromis* and *Sarotherodon*.

Apart from fisheries which use macrophyte stands for spawning, rearing and feeding, littoral zones of lakes are the most productive systems in the world (Pieczynska, 1990). The lake littoral zone is utilised by many species of birds; Lake Jipe is an important feeding and nesting site for avifauna, and other lakes are important for migratory birds (Stuart, 1990).

In addition to providing an important source of protein, lakes are also important in the socio-economic activities of people. They provide employment, sport and transport; they supply water for livestock, domestic use and irrigation. Vegetation growing on lake margins, such as *Cyperus papyrus*, is used to produce mats, rafts, baskets and decorations.

Rivers

The network of rivers in Tanzania (see Figure 3 in the Introduction) constitutes one of the country's richest and most dependable resources. Rivers support important activities including fishing, transport and provision of water for domes- tic purposes, irrigation and livestock. Riverine fish include *Schilbe mystus* (butterfish, 'nembe'), *Labeo victorianus* ('ningu'), *Barbus altianalis radcliffii* ('kuyu') and *Alestes jacksonii* ('soga').

The Kagera and Rufiji Rivers are navigable by large vessels for significant distances but most rivers in Tanzania are only navigable by canoe.

The Kilombero River floodplain is inhabited by a variety of wildlife such as crocodiles, hippopotamus, various antelopes, elephant and buffalo (Semesi, 1989). Floodplains are important in groundwater recharge and discharge; flood control; sediment, toxicant and nutrient retention; and export of biomass (Dugan, 1990; Table 1). Most of these functions are carried out by floodplains in the Rufiji River basin, especially Usangu, Kilombero and the lower Rufiji plains.

Marshes and swamps

Marshes are characterised by herbaceous plants and sustained by water sources other than direct rainfall. Swamps may develop in areas of still water around lake margins and in parts of floodplains, such as sloughs or oxbows (Maltby, 1986). These areas have a rich and diverse flora and fauna. The Bahi Swamp is an important breeding site for birds and fish. The Malagarasi-Moyowosi System and its southern extension into the Ugalla Game Reserve, are sources of fish and other wetland products. The Wembere Swamps have large nesting colonies of water birds, while wetlands in the Selous Game Reserve support substantial numbers of wildlife and fish. Swamps, especially those outside reserves are important for agricultural production, especially rice.

Estuaries

Estuaries are among the most fertile areas in the world, with micro- and macro-flora and fauna maintaining high productivity. Odum (1971) attributes the high productivity of estuaries to the following:

1. Capacity to trap nutrients either physically or biologically. This characteristic predisposes the system to eutrophication and vulnerability to pollution.
2. Habitats for the three producers (macrophytes, benthic microphytes and phytoplankton).
3. Tidal movement of water which removes wastes and transports food and nutrients so that organisms can maintain a sessile existence.

Estuaries and deltas are dynamic, responding to changes in the upper catchment areas and the shoreline. In the Rufiji Delta, some channels are increasing in activity while others are decreasing.

Mangrove forests

Mangroves characterise estuarine ecosystems; they are important economic resources of the coastal people of Tanzania and are utilised as sources of firewood, poles, and timber for construction of canoes, boats and dhows. The mangroves are feeding, breeding and nursery grounds for many fish species (Semesi, 1989; Bwathondi and Ngoile, 1990) and they support a variety of insects, birds and other small animals. In the Rufiji Delta, four villages produced 6,300 kg of honey and 802 kg of wax in 1987 (Semesi, 1989). There is some potential for tourism in the mangrove forests, especially where navigable channels allow travel from the ocean to terrestrial ecosystems.

Mangroves provide protection from storms, act as wind breaks, control soil erosion, stabilise shorelines and enhance water quality in coastal streams and estuaries.

Conservation of wetlands in Tanzania

There is lack of detailed information and data on the importance of wetlands in Tanzania but there is considerable concern that entire aquatic ecosystems are now under threat (Dugan, 1990).

Reasons for conservation

Perceived reasons leading to wetland degradation include: the disruption of these ecosystems by reservoir construction; interfering with catchment areas; agricultural intensification; extensive livestock husbandry; agro-chemical and other pollution; indiscriminate urban development; deforestation; and mining practices.

21

Several authors have highlighted wetland deterioration worldwide (Maltby, 1986; Dugan, 1989; NEMC/WWF/IUCN, 1990). In Tanzania, both human activities and natural threats such as sea level rise, drought, storms and erosion contribute to wetland degradation.

There is already an outcry against the consequence of human activities in wetlands, including the serious beach erosion along the coast; the loss of Lake Haubi in Kondoa; drastic reduction of waterlilies in the Kagera River; the silting of the Little and Great Ruaha River complex; drying of the lower streams on Mt Kilimanjaro; drying of many rivers, swamps and marshes; pollution of rivers and lakes (MWEM, 1991); and vigorous growth of water hyacinth in Lake Victoria and the Pangani River.

Many reasons can be advanced for conserving Tanzania's wetlands. The rural economy in many parts of the country is dependent on wetlands for fish protein, pasture for livestock, crop production and water sources. Tanzania is rich and diverse in terms of both species and habitats and is renown for her endemic species. Wetlands are important as habitats for biodiversity and endemic species.

Proposed wetlands for conservation

Many wetlands are conserved in the game reserves, national parks, Ngorongoro Conservation Area and the controlled areas, while others have no conservation status. Wetlands need to be conserved because of their fragility, endemic nature, historical importance, functions, products and attributes. In Table 3, some of the important wetlands areas for conservation are identified.

Problems facing wetland management

Institutional weakness

The management of wetlands is the responsibility of many institutions in Tanzania. The lack of coordination between these institutions has resulted in poor management, lack of accountability, inability to respond to changes in wetlands, and failure to partition responsibilities between institutions.

Sectoral management

Different users see different attributes in wetlands (Dugan, 1990). Agriculturalists see moist, fertile soils with vast potential for growing rice, maize, sorghum and cotton; fishery managers find a potential for fish production; hydrologists calculate water supply and demand for various projects; foresters are interested in the mangroves and riverine forests; game wardens view wetlands as sanctuaries for wildlife; ecologists are interested in the intricacies of the ecosystems; health specialists look at wetlands as regulators of water quality or sources of diseases; and TANESCO engineers see them as cheap sources of electricity.

Table 3   Wetland areas proposed for conservation

Wetland	Importance/values	Status/remarks
Mangrove forests	Mutiple values: fish feeding, breeding and nursery areas	Declared forest reserves; threatened species
Rufiji Delta	Multiple values	Integrated approach needed. Already resources are depleted
Wembere Swamps	Multi-purpose use	Bird nesting colonies
Lake Natron	Flamingo breeding ground	Could be tourist attraction
Bahi Swamps	Bird breeding ground	Could be utilised for fish protein in Central Tanzania
Kagera Swamp	Important for fish and bird nesting	Much siltation; needs inter-regional planning and use
Marine parks	Coral gardens, fish breeding, bird nesting and feeding, tourism, rare and endangered species, educational and scientific areas	There is human pressure; cutting mangroves, depletion of corals, construction along coastline, beach erosion, pollution

Wetlands are often viewed by each user as a single-product system, precluding other uses and values. It is important to understand that wetlands are multi-functional and their management should be integrated and coordinated. Planning at sectoral level should be harmonised.

Legislative problems

Wetland management needs effective legislation, which takes into account the diverse nature of wetlands and is supported by effective enforcement and re-sources. This legislation must take into account the needs of wetlands and the requirement of all the sectors that use them.

Lack of qualified manpower

There is serious lack of trained manpower to manage wetlands. Greater inter-disciplinary skills are needed by wetland managers than managers of most other natural resources. The type of training for wetland management should cover a broad spectrum of knowledge. Examples of overly narrow training follow:

- irrigation engineers trained in water management rather than in maximising the contribution of aquatic systems to human needs;
- resource planners trained to manage different natural resources and habitats as discrete units rather than crossing administrative boundaries;
- foresters trained in forest management rather than going beyond to understand the ecological inter-dependencies.

Limited resources

Adequate funds are needed for staffing, purchase of equipment, construction of infrastructure, and running of logistics.

Limited information database

There exists a bias which favours development of wetlands and thus degradation of wetland ecosystems. The non-market values of wetland attributes are seldom considered while products (fish, meat, skin, poles, crops) carry monetary value.

Limited research projects are carried out in wetlands and existing data and is not made public or shared between sectors.

There is a lack of appreciation by the public, policy makers, planners and developers of the overall values and benefits of wetlands. Both community leaders and the citizens of Tanzania should be made aware of the values of wetlands and the proper management of these endowments.

Lack of policy on wetland management

Efforts to conserve wetlands may be ineffectual because of competing government priorities and interests. Thus one department or organisation may devote resources to wetland conservation while another is promoting wetland development. A national wetland policy would iron out these anomalies.

Conclusion

There is a consensus that wetlands are, and should remain, important ecological systems in Tanzania. There are many diverse wetland systems in Tanzania yet the nation has failed to appreciate their values. The treasure harboured by these wetlands is gradually being eroded and there is an urgent need for the restoration of already degraded wetlands and the conservation of those which are threatened.

As the population increases, and thus more demands are made on resources, wetlands may be further destroyed in the name of development. Development should be avoided if the cost is environmental degradation.

Bibliography

Bureau of Statistics. 1989. Statistical Abstract 1987. The Planning Commission. United Republic of Tanzania.

Bwathondi, P.O.J. 1990. The State of Fishing industry in Tanzania with particular reference to inland fishery. *Proceeding of a Seminar on Prevailing Activities on the Lake Victoria Basin*, 8-9 March, 1990. pp. 5-8.

Bwathondi, P.O.J. and M.A.K. Ngoile. 1990. Environmental aspects of the utilization of aquatic research. Pages 185-208. In: A. Kauzeni, H.F. Bitanyi and M.A.K. Ngoile (Eds). *Proceeding of Seminar on National Conservation Strategy for Tanzania*. 12-17 November, 1990. Dodoma. NEMC, SIDA.

Dugan, P.J. (Ed.) 1990. *Wetland Conservation: A review of current issues and required action*. IUCN, Gland, Switzerland. 96 pp.

Kamukala, G.L. 1990. Issues and Opportunities for Wetland Conservation in East Africa: the Case of Tanzania. Paper presented to the IUCN General Assembly, Perth, Australia. 28 November - 5 December 1990.

Kurata, A. and T. Kira. 1990. Water quality aspects. Pages 21-36. In: S.E. Jorgensen and H. Hoffler (Eds). *Guidelines of Lake Management*. Vol.3. ILEC and UNEP, Otsu, Japan.

Land Resources Development Centre (LRDC) and Overseas Development Agency (ODA), Surbiton, UK. Unpublished report.

LRDC and ODA. 1987. Tanzania: Profile of Agricultural Potential.

Maltby, E. 1986. *Waterlogged Wealth: Why Waste the World's Wet Places?* International Institute for Environment and Development. London. 200 pp.

MWEM. 1991. Report by Principal Secretary, Ministry of Water, Energy and Minerals (MWEM). *Daily News* 19-22 March, 1991.

NEMC/WWF/IUCN. 1990. *Development of a Wetland Conservation and Management Programme for Tanzania*. IUCN, Gland, Switzerland. 113 pp.

Odum, E.P. 1971. *Fundamentals of Ecology*. W.B. Saunders, Philadelphia, USA.

Pieczynska, E. 1990. Littoral habitats and communities. Pages 45-66. In: S.E. Jorgensen and H. Hoffer (Eds). *Guidelines of Lake Management*. Vol. 3. ILEC and UNEP, Otsu, Japan.

Semesi, A.K. 1988. Status and utilisation of mangroves along the coast of Tanga, Tanzania. Pages 174-180. In: J.R. Mainoya (Ed.). *Proceeding of a seminar on Ecology and Bioproductivity of the Marine Coastal Waters of Eastern Africa*, 18-20 January. University of Dar es Salaam.

Semesi, A.K. 1989. Conserving the mangrove forests of East Africa: the Case of the Rufiji Delta Mangrove, Tanzania. Paper presented to a workshop on Marine Sciences in East Africa. 14-16 November, 1989. Dar es Salaam.

Simmons, I.G. 1981. *The Ecology of Natural Resources*. Edward Arnold, London.

Stuart, S.N. 1990. The Threats to Biodiversity and Genetic Resources in Tanzania. Pages 238-9. In: A. Kauzeni, H.F. Bitanyi and M.A.K. Ngoile (Eds). *Proceeding of seminar on National Conservation Strategy for Tanzania*, 12-17 November, 1990. Dodoma. NEMC, SIDA.

Origin and geomorphology of the wetlands of Tanzania

P.P.K. Mwanukuzi

Geography Department
University of Dar es Salaam
P.O. Box 35049
Dar es Salaam

Summary

Wetlands are dynamic landforms which vary in both time and space. Tanzania's wetlands are classified according to the physiography and the environment in which they exist. Coastal wetlands, Rift System wetlands and the wetlands of highland drainage basins are the major groups. Coastal wetlands are formed by wave action and tidal influence; beaches and lagoons exist because of wave action; mudflats, marshes, mangrove swamps, estuaries and deltas are tidal in origin. Rift System wetlands occur in the rift depressions and are characterised by salt lakes, playas, swamps and short streams with inland drainage. The highlands are drained by long rivers originating in the inland catchments and ending in oceans or lake basins. On the way to their outlets, they form lakes, swamps and floodplains.

Wetlands occur due to a combination of high rainfall and the tropical climate of Tanzania which favours processes such as meandering of rivers and the formation of floodplains. The morphogenesis of Tanzania's wetlands is related not only to local processes but also to regional factors such as climate, tectonism and the eustatic sea level changes which occurred in the past.

Introduction

Natural wetlands are dynamic and short lived in geological time and have vanished and emerged since the formation of the earth. Areas which now supply limestone, coal, peat, phosphate, salts (evaporites) and diatomite were once wetlands. Today's wetlands are a source of food and cash but unfortunately also disease.

Tanzania's morphology has resulted from the interplay between geology and the tropical climate. Her position close to the equator means that winds are light. In the tropics, chemical weathering predominates and results in a preponderance of fine material and clays; weathering is rapid, resulting in a deep weathering front.

27

This paper explains the origin of the present natural wetlands of Tanzania. A general classification of Tanzanian wetlands is used to accommodate their diversity of formation and the morphogenetics of Tanzanian wetlands are discussed in terms of regional climate and tectonism.

Categories of Tanzanian wetlands

The natural wetlands of Tanzania are grouped into three categories according to their origins and land physiography. The definition of wetlands used in this paper follows that of the Ramsar Convention (see Introduction).

The first category is the coastal wetlands, which are coastal landforms, permanently or temporarily occupied by water. Examples include beaches, mudflats, salt marshes, mangrove swamps, estuaries, coastal deltas and coastal floodplains which lie less than 15 m above sea level and which are directly influenced by the sea processes. The Rift System wetlands are the second category. They were formed as a result of rifting or formed in structures influenced by rifting and volcanism. This group includes lakes, pools, ponds, swamps surrounding the Rift Lakes, or ponds and other wetlands supplied by springs and streams associated with the Rift System. The third category includes the rivers and inland floodplains draining hinterland basins and terminating in oceans or in the large East African lakes.

Development and geomorphology of coastal wetlands

The present Tanzanian shoreline was formed after the last ice age (10,000 years ago). The world climate has alternated between the cold climatic periods, the ice ages, and the warm climatic periods or inter-ice ages. Water was drawn from the sea during ice formation, resulting in a sea level fall; while the melting of ice added water to the interconnected oceans, causing the sea level to rise. As a result of the end of the last ice age, sea levels stopped rising 6,000 years ago. Thus the present sea outline is the result of such historical changes. However, since the establishment of a shoreline, the sea, through continuous tidal and wave action, has produced the present coastal landforms.

There are sea level changes unrelated to historical ice ages. Within the past century, sea level change has occurred within a band of -0.5 to +22 cm (Houghton *et al.*, 1990), attributed to the melting of low latitude glaciers and Antarctic ice, and thermal expansion of the ocean, as the result of global warming. This change is too small to have a significant effect on coastal topography and coastal landforms are formed by daily changes of the sea level resulting from the interplay between tides and waves. At a particular site, specific coastal landforms occur depending on the relative dominance between tidal currents and waves caused by wind.

Wetlands formed by wind waves

A beach is a gently sloping accumulation of sand or shingles, between low water spring tide and the highest point reached by wind waves. The sediments of a beach are well sorted because of the continuous winnowing by waves. Such material is supplied from local cliffs and other promontories, the offshore zone, dead organisms such as corals, molluscs, diatoms, and from sediments carried to the coast by rivers.

The beach profile

The beach profile depends on both the size of the beach sediments and the nature of waves reaching the shore. Coarse grain, sandy or shingle beaches tend to be steeper, with higher percolation rates, than those composed of fine sands. When a surge of wave water reaches the former type of beach, most of the water percolates through the sands thus reducing the volume of the backwash and producing a steep beach. On fine sand beaches, the percolation rate is low and the amount of water in the swash and backwash is almost equal. As a result, the same amount of sediments deposited on the beach by swash water are also eroded by the backwash and the beach tends to be relatively flat (King, 1972).

The type of breaking wave which dominates the shore will effect the beach slope. The wave breaking zone depends on wave height and depth of water, for instance in shallow water waves collapse far away from the shoreline. In order of increasing height, waves are classified as surging, collapsing, plunging or spilling. Surging breakers run close to the shore before breaking and push sands up towards the beach berm, resulting in a steep beach. On the other hand, spilling breakers become unstable in deep water and only a thin layer of water foam reaches the shore with insufficient energy to push the sand towards the berm, resulting in a flat beach.

Detached beaches and lagoons

Detached beaches enclose sea water to form lagoons and may form barrier islands. A rise in sea level, resulting in the drowning of beach berms, the movement of sand bars on-shore, or the formation and extension of spits results in the formation of barrier islands. Spits are formed by longshore drift, caused by the action of oblique waves striking the shoreline. When an oblique wave reaches a deeply indented headland bay sequence, wave refraction causes an energy gradient along the shore with a shadow of low energy in the bay. Sediments build outward from the headland shore and enclose the bay to form a lagoon (Swift, 1976). Coastal lagoons in Tanzania may be formed by spit enclosure or by the formation of coral reef barriers.

Wetlands formed by tidal changes

Hayes (1975) distinguished between tidal landforms and wind wave landforms and assumed that coastal areas which experience tidal ranges in excess of 4 m are dominated by tidal landforms. These landforms, caused by horizontal shift of material by the tides, are mudflats, salt marshes and mangrove swamps. When the tides interact with a river, an estuary or delta forms.

Mudflats and their morphology

Mudflats consist of fine grained silts and clay and are found between low tide and maximum high tide in areas sheltered from the open sea by barrier islands or sand bars. Aerial photographs show that mudflats dominate in Tanga District, from Kilanje Creek at Mtangata Bay northwards to the Kenya border. Southwards, mudflats with their backswamps support 16.5 km^2 of mangroves in Mtwara within the shelter of Mnanka Island. In Nangurukuru, the Mavunji creek has mudflats and swamps covering a total area of 62 km^2. The Mnazi Bay mudflats are sheltered from the open sea by the fringing coral reefs of Ras Mpura and Ras Mawala.

Mudflats slope gently (1:1,000 gradient) towards the sea (Pethick, 1984). The grain size of sediments on the mudflats decreases progressively towards the land. Upper mudflats are covered by water only at high tide; at the mid-tide level the slope increases and the deposited material becomes progressively more sandy towards the low tide mark. The spacial distribution of sediment size on mudflats and their morphology is explained by tidal wave movement. As the tidal flow moves landwards up the gently sloping mudflat, its velocity increases from zero, at low tide, to a maximum at mid-tide and back to zero at high tide when the entire mudflat is submerged. Coarser sediments settle as soon as the velocity starts to fall; sands settle more rapidly than clays. Most sediments are deposited landward because of fine sediment concentration and settling lag, thus the height of mudflats rises more quickly on the shoreward surfaces than on the offshore surfaces. Mudflats within creeks and sheltered by barriers rise from the creek towards the land.

Development of marshes and swamps

Salt marshes can be defined as vegetated mudflats which occur at a higher level, relative to mean tide level. Marshes are usually flooded only by the highest spring tides. As the mudflat grows, a critical point is reached when duration of tidal flooding decreases and the increased exposure allows vegetation to colonise the area. Factors influencing the colonisation of mudflats to form marshes include:
–   the availability of suitable plant species able to withstand such a difficult environment;
–   low velocity of the tidal current allowing plant seedlings to anchor on the mudflats;
–   the availability of light for plant growth which, in turn, depends on the duration of tidal flooding and turbidity and salinity of tidal water.

Swamps are permanently inundated marshes. Swamps may develop from marshes if there is a relative change between the sea and land levels, such as a rise of sea level or subsidence of land, and consequent sea transgression. The marshes of Tanzania are covered by salt tolerant grass and scattered trees. Salt panning usually takes place on coastal marshes.

Mangrove swamps are found in creeks, estuaries, deltas and closed embayments where the influence of salt water prevails. Significant mangrove swamps occur at the mouth of the Rufiji River in the Coast Region, Ruvuma River around the Letoko distributary, and Kisiju near Bagamoyo.

Estuaries and coastal deltas

An estuary is the mouth of a river where a channel broadens out into a trumpet-like shape and within which the tide flows and ebbs. The shape of the estuary depends on the tidal range of the sea. A small tidal range results in a bar-built estuary where riverine sediments plug the river mouth, preventing the tidal flow from entering the river channel. A bay or lagoon forms where both river and seawater mix.

Drowned river valleys result when the rising sea levels submerge the river channel. Rias are formed when a deeply bisected area has been drowned and the resulting estuaries are steep sided and penetrate far inland.

Estuarine processes

The tidal current and river discharge influence the estuarine processes; those which control sediment transportation are the most fundamental to estuarine morphology. As the tidal wave enters the estuary, the velocity of the tidal current increases to a maximum at mid-tide, when only the central channel of the estuary is affected, and is at a minimum at high tide, when the suspended load settles in the upper part of the estuary. Thus more sediment is carried into the estuary than out and the upper part of the estuary becomes a sediment trap. High discharges by the fluvial channel occur during seasonal floods which are less frequent than tidal floods. Mudflats in the upper estuary accrete faster than lower mudflats.

A high tidal range, greater than 4 m, produces a funnel-shaped estuary. As the tidal wave moves upstream it loses energy rapidly because of friction, thus the seaward side of the channel is eroded wider than upstream.

Mixing of fresh and saline waters also controls sediment deposition in the estuary. High tidal range and low river discharge facilitate water mixing. As dense salt water moves into the estuary and mixes with fresh water there is a loss of volume and more seawater enters the estuary to compensate. The resulting residue current moves sediment to the estuary.

If mixing of salt water and freshwater is not substantial, a salt wedge penetrates the estuary. Freshwater rises over the salt wedge, leaving its bed load at the tip of the salt wedge. The suspended load moves towards the sea and is deposited as the velocity falls. This occurs when the flow of the river is high and tidal range is small; suspended sediment is deposited towards the sea resulting in the formation of a delta.

A typical estuarine environment is found where the Pangani River enters the Indian Ocean at Pangani Bay (Figure 1). The Pangani estuary is macro-tidal and has a typical funnel shape. At the entrance of the Rufiji River a delta has formed as a result of high sediment and fluvial water input and low tidal range. Sediments move offshore and wave currents redistribute the sediment over a wide, shallow

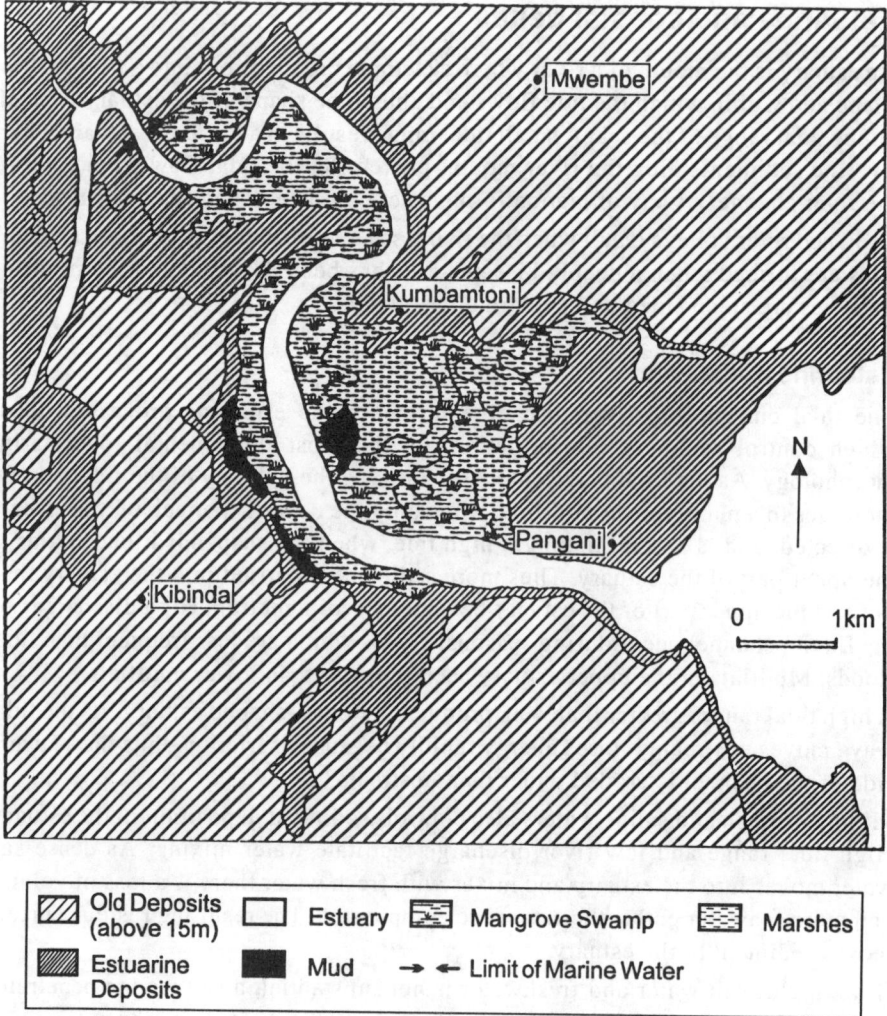

Figure 1   Extension of the Pangani estuary. The boundary between the land
covered by old deposits and the estuarine deposits traces the drowned
river valley, after the major rising of the sea level

area into which the delta is advancing. The deltaic flat land of the Rufiji River, approximately 1,400 km^2, is covered by swamps and marshes which form a large wetland. A similar but smaller situation is found at the mouth of Ruvuma River in Mtwara Region.

Tanzanian Rift System wetlands

Any process which produces a depression in the landscape may lead to wetland formation if water supply and the nature of underlaying formations allow. Rifting and volcanism produce depressions and lines of weakness for water accumulation. Rifting, the result of faulting and upwarping, produces horsts, grabens or titled blocks which are curved by erosion to produce erosional and deposition sites for water accumulation. Faulting forms lines of weakness by shearing and shattering rocks; weathering and erosion then readily occurs and forms drainage lines.

Volcanic eruptions form craters and calderas. These circular depressive features may collect water and develop wetlands. Volcanism and faulting acts not only as the shaping agent of the earth's surface for accumulation of rain but can also supply water to the surface from deep sources. Some crater lakes are seen in Rungwe, Basotu and in the Ngorongoro Crater.

The East Africa Rift covers extensive parts of Tanzania. The system of troughs and faults runs southwards from Lake Natron to Dodoma in the Bahi depression (6°10'S) and varies in width from 30 km to 90 km. On the western side, the Rift System covers the basin of Lake Nyasa, through Mbeya and Rukwa, to Lake Tanganyika. The wetlands in this area are lakes, short rivers, swamps and marshes. Typical examples of the small lakes with associated swamps are Lakes Natron, Eyasi, Manyara, Rukwa and Balangida. These lakes are bounded by fault scarps and, as they have no outlets, their waters are saline. Short rivers entering these lakes originate from tilted or upthrusted blocks in the Rift Valley. Some contain swamps in depressions; the Wembere River drains into Lake Eyasi, the Bubu River drains into the Bahi depression, and a number of small streams flow into Lake Rukwa.

The Rift Valley lakes fluctuate in size and consequently form playas and swamps on their fringes. Large areas of old Lake Rukwa have become swamps. The change in size of the lake may occur due to progressive infilling of the lake basin by sediments, change of climate, tectonic activity causing uplift and subsidence, or the development of drainage faults.

Faults in the Rift System are associated with deep seated springs which can be characterised by the temperature and salinity of the water (James, 1967). These springs may result in the formation of streams and swamps, such as the Itembu and Manyengi Swamps in Central Tanzania.

Wetlands of the highlands drainage basins

Highland drainage wetlands include the swamps and floodplains of the major rivers of Tanzania which originate in the highlands with high rainfall. The Pangani River drains the Kilimanjaro-Usambara uplands; the Wami River is fed from the Unguru Hills and part of central plateau; the Rufiji River, the largest in Tanzania, drains the southern highlands through its main tributaries the Little Ruaha, Greater Ruaha and Kilombero. In western Tanzania, the Malagarasi River has extensive swamps and floodplains along its valley and the Kagera River drains into Lake Victoria through the Kyaka, Minziro and Mwemange Swamps.

River channel morphology

Erosion, transportation and deposition by flowing water interact with underlying structures, lithology and land morphology to determine the shape of a river channel. Important features of the Tanzania rivers are meanders, braids, floodplains and backswamps.

Floodplains form when a river passes through low lying land and sediments accumulate by lateral migration of the river channel or by overbank deposition from flood water. Lateral migration occurs on both braided and meandering channels; the latter forms ox-bow lakes which eventually fill by overbank flow; braided channels form when a river is overloaded with bed material so that deposition occurs to form braid bars. If the river bank is easily eroded, the river meanders due to the infilling of older channels and erosion of new channels. Overflow during flooding causes accumulation of sediments on the banks to form barriers called levees. Levees may grow above the floodplain and areas between the levees and valley walls then become poorly drained, leading to the formation of backswamps.

The major Tanzanian rivers have floodplains in their lower reaches, including the Rufiji, Ruvuma and Kagera Rivers. Striking features of the Rufiji River are meanders and ox-bow lakes (Figure 2). The Ruvuma River is characterised by a braided channel with a narrow floodplain. A large swamp occurs on the Malagarasi River, situated between the mobile belt and the craton, which may represent an area where rocks, weakened by folding and faulting, were selectively eroded and depressed.

Discussion and conclusion

The processes of wetland formation discussed in this paper are those found in Tanzania. However, some regional factors may also contribute to the formation of observed features. For example, beach sediments found on the Tanzania coast may be related to the process of weathering far inland. Due to a tropical climate with high humidity, weathering is essentially chemical and sediments originating from chemical weathering are usually of fine texture. These sediments are supplied to

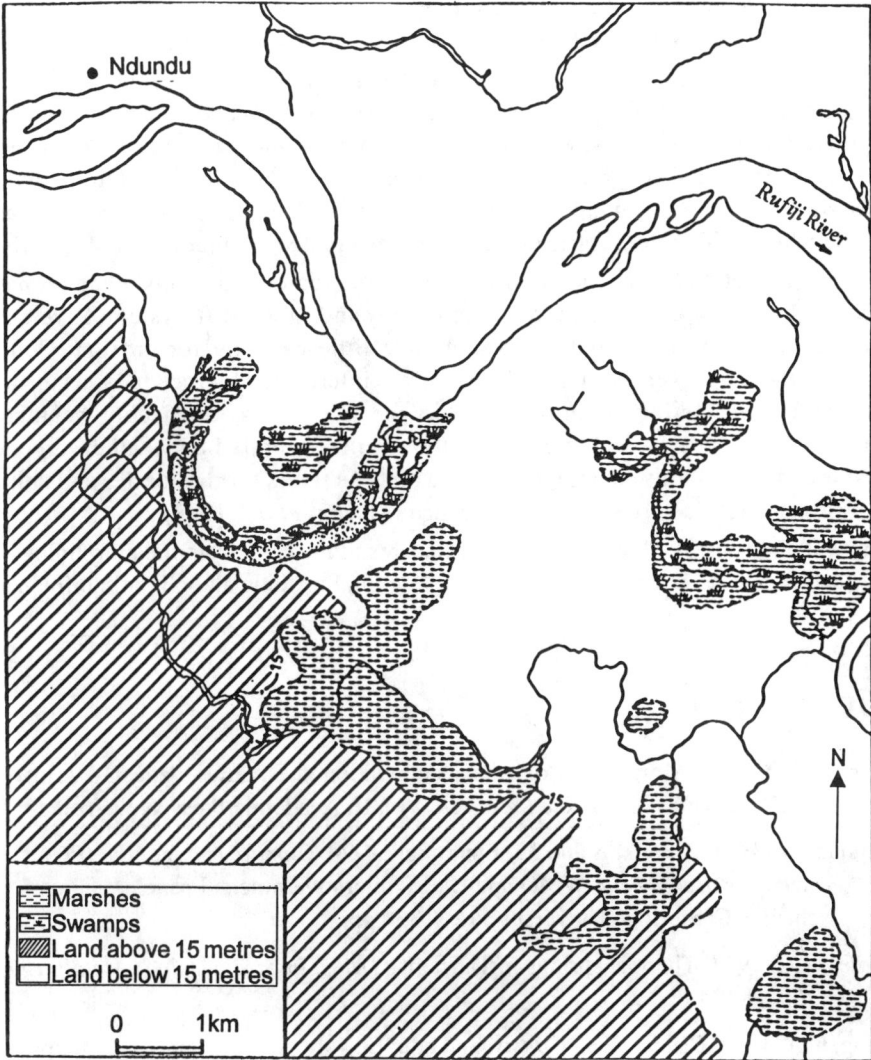

Figure 2   The lower Rufiji River floodplain at Ndundu, Rufiji District. The main river channel has migrated northwards, abandoning the older loops, left as ox-bow lakes, swamps and marshes

the coast by rivers and influence beach gradient. Therefore, the gently sloping beaches along the coast of Tanzania are a consequence of the interaction between climate and the rocks in the hinterland.

The small amount of sand carried by Tanzania's rivers, as a result of the preponderance of chemical weathering, accounts for the absence of large sand landforms on the Tanzanian coast, such as coastal lagoons with sand barriers.

The tropical climate favours the growth of coral which forms lagoons behind a coralline barrier reef. The creeks along the Tanzanian coast demonstrate the effect of tidal dominance over waves. Low wave energy along the Tanzania coast may be traced from its geographical position as Tanzania, being near the equator, experiences only light winds and no cyclones; absence of strong winds favours gentle waves which do not travel far into creeks to disrupt mudflat configuration.

The inland wetlands have been influenced by the regional tectonism and climate. Enclosed water bodies and short streams are found in the Rift System. Rivers are loaded with fine grains and sands and have little capacity for erosion. Consequently, the long rivers from the highlands are interrupted by rock bars, waterfalls and rapids. On the low lying lands, rivers meander across the deeply weathered plains and, since they cannot erode all the regolith supplied by weathering, open basins and floodplains emerge. On the coast, these rivers form estuaries and deltas. Tanzanian estuaries are sites of subsidence (Msangi *et al.*, 1988).

The wetlands observed on the earth's surface result not only from the morphology of the land in which they occur but are due to regional tectonic and climatic influence.

Bibliography

Hayes, M.O. 1975. Morphology of sand accumulation in estuaries. Pages 3-22. In: L. Cronin (Ed.). *Estuarine Research*. Vol. II. Academic Press, New York.

Houghton, J.H., G.J. Jenkins and J.J. Ephraums. 1990. *Climate change: the IPCC scientific assessment.* WMO and UNEP intergovernmental panel on climate change. Cambridge University Press. 364 pp.

James, T.C. 1967. Thermal springs in Tanzania. *Trans. Inst. Mineralogy Metallurgy* 76:168-174.

King, C.A. 1972. *Beaches and Coasts*. 2nd edn. Edward Arnold, London. 570 pp.

Msangi, J.P., C.J. Grifiths and W.F. Banyikwa. 1988. Man's response to change in the coastal zone of Tanzania. Pages 37-60. In: K. Ruddle, W.B. Morgan and J.R. Plafflin (Eds). *The Coastal Zone: Man's Response to Change*. Chur, Harwood.

Pethick, J. 1984. *An Introduction to Coastal Geomorphology*. Edward Arnold, London. 260 pp.

Swift, D.J.P. 1976. Coastal sedimentation. In: D.J. Stanley and D.J.P. Swift (Eds). *Marine Sediment Transport and Environmental Management*. Wiley, New York.

Forestry resources in Tanzania's wetlands: concepts and potentials

L. Nshubemuki

Tanzania Forestry Research Institute
P.O. Box 1854
Morogoro

Summary

Forestry resources include land occupied by, or proclaimed to be forest; the produce found in such land; and human resources capable of fostering the development of such resources. The following landscape units constitute Tanzania's wetlands: estuaries, open coasts, wetlands in coastal forests, floodplains, freshwater marshes, lakes, peatlands, swamp forests, and ground water forests.

Wetlands are sources of food and forest produce, contain plants potentially suitable for agro-forestry and phyto-reclamation, reduce beach erosion, and are sources of genetic material. Most wetlands face intensive utilisation pressure which endangers their continued existence. Given the multi-utility of wetlands and their diversity in structure, it is not possible to adopt a single conservation strategy. The ecosystem approach to conservation, incorporating the preservation of genetic and ecological diversity alongside scientific research, environmental monitoring, education and training, is advocated in preference to traditional conservation.

Public awareness of the uniqueness of Tanzania's flora and fauna needs to be strengthened as this should guarantee the long term protection of wetlands.

Introduction

Forestry resources are, in essence, forestry assets. Economists define an asset as that which is owned and has a monetary value. Assets may be fixed (buildings and machinery), liquid (cash), intangible (goodwill) or current (goods in stock, cash and bills) (Ford-Robertson, 1971). Extending this definition to forestry, assets include land occupied by, or proclaimed to be forest, the produce found in such land, and the incommensurable human resources capable of fostering the development of such resources.

In Tanzania, forest produce (Forest Ordinance No. 30 of 1957, Cap. 389) includes:
- trees, timber, firewood, charcoal, sawdust, withies, bark, roots, fibres, resins, gums, latex, sap, galls, leaves, fruits and seeds; and
- within forest reserves only; vegetation of any kind, litter, soil, peat, honey, wax and wild silk; and
- such other things as the Governor may from time to time by notice published in the gazette declare to be forest produce, either generally or within any forest reserve.

In forestry law, the term tree includes: palms, bamboos, canes, shrubs, bushes, plants, poles, climbers, seedlings, saplings, and regrowth of all kinds. It follows that forestry resources encompass a wide range of items.

Wetlands cover a range of inland, coastal and marine habitats which share a number of common features. The range of wetland habitats which come under the mandate of the Ramsar Convention on Wetlands of International Importance especially as Wildfowl Habitat is impressive. Crude grouping of habitat types according to their basic biological and physical characteristics gives 30 categories of natural and 9 of man-made wetlands. In this paper, only landscape units which are wetlands, or where wetlands form an important component, are considered; these are estuaries, open coasts, coastal forest wetlands, floodplains, lakes, freshwater marshes, peatlands, swamp forests, and groundwater forests.

Importance of Tanzanian wetlands

Wetlands have standing water for at least part of the year. This leads to the view that they are wastelands and that they should be filled in or drained so that they could be put to better use. Recently, informed public opinion and land and water management agencies of governments, notably in the United States, have taken the view that the world's remaining wetlands are more useful in preventing floods, recharging groundwater, controlling pollution and providing habitats and breeding grounds for fish and wildlife (Botts, 1982).

A significant amount of Tanzania's rice is obtained from the floodplains located in Mwanza, Shinyanga, Tabora, Mbeya, Morogoro and Coast Regions. The Wembere, Bahi and Malagarasi Swamps are important sources of fish. Estuaries, such as those of the Rufiji, Wami and Ruvuma Rivers and other coastal wetlands, are among the most productive environments in the world, acting as nurseries for valuable fisheries. Mangrove roots and branches diminish the effects of ocean waves and reduce beach erosion. The Kilombero and Kagera Swamps produce a significant proportion of Tanzania's sugar. In Iringa Region, Mbuga Swamps mitigate floods by retaining water and allowing groundwater recharge. The trapping of sediment by wetlands influences the output of hydroelectricity and the maintenance of riparian ecosystems downstream.

The swamps bordering the Malagarasi River play a significant role in the maintenance of biodiversity within Lake Tanganyika which contains one of the largest faunas (in terms of species) of any lake in the world. Over 1,300 species of invertebrates have been described from Lake Tanganyika, of which well over 500 are endemic. Distinct and diverse communities exist in the pelagic, benthic, and littoral biotopes (Cohen, 1991; Coulter, 1991). Lake Tanganyika is a rare natural laboratory where ecological, biological, behavioural and evolutionary mechanisms can be studied (Lowe-McConnell, 1991). The trapping of sediment resulting from deforestation of the lake's catchment, is a significant contribution of wetlands to the maintenance of the lake's biodiversity.

The shores of the Rift Valley lakes provide excellent habitats for birds; flamingos are found in Lake Manyara, which is a major attraction to bird watchers in Tanzania. Mangrove vegetation, found in estuaries, provides feeding, roosting and breeding sites for birds.

It is difficult to assign a monetary value to the wetland attributes outlined above. As a part of an ecosystem, a wetland provides many functions that act together to increase its value. Tanzanian wetlands have value for agriculture, fisheries, wild-life, maintenance of biodiversity, and flood control. Considered as a biological system, rather than in terms of separate benefits, the ecosystem approach must be pursued in an effort to secure understanding of the complex interrelationships found in wetlands.

The vegetation of Tanzania's wetlands

The potentials of Tanzanian wetlands are presented under the nine landscape units mentioned above.

Estuaries

An estuaries is a body of water where a river mouth widens into a marine ecosystem, where the salinity alternates between salt and fresh water, and where tidal action is an important bio-physical regulator. Estuaries and inshore marine waters are among the most naturally fertile ecosystems in the world. This high productivity supports a food web which permits rapid growth of the juvenile fish which use estuaries as nursery areas.

Tropical and sub-tropical estuaries support mangrove vegetation and occasionally palms in higher latitudes (Chapman, 1976). Physiographic features that favour the development of mangroves include protected shallow bays; protected or unpro-tected estuaries; lagoons; the leeward side of peninsulas and islands; protected seaways; protected areas on offshore shell or shingle islands (Banyikwa, 1986). In Tanzania, there are around 115,500 ha of mangroves with the majority (53,255 ha) occurring in the Rufiji Delta; of the 40.8 million hectares classified as forests in Tanzania, mangrove forests occupy less than 1%.

A review of mangrove distribution in East Africa is given by Banyikwa (1986). Different mangrove community structures occurring in Tanzania have been described

Table 1   Potential economic uses of mangroves

Uses	A. marina	B. gymnorrhiza	C. tagal	H. littoralis	R. mucronata	S. alba	X. granatum
Beams	+	+	+	-	-	-	+
Boat building	-	+	+	-	-	+	+
Poles	+	+	+	+	+	+	+
Carving	-	-	-	-	-	-	+
Charcoal	-	+	-	+	-	-	+
Chipboard	+	+	-	-	+	-	-
Jetty beams	-	-	-	+	+	+	-
Dye	-	-	+	+	+	+	+
Fence posts	-	+	-	+	+	+	+
Firewood	+	+	+	+	+	+	+
Floats	-	-	-	-	+	+	+
Fodder	-	-	-	-	-	+	-
Furniture	-	+	-	+	+	+	+
Green manure	+	-	-	-	+	+	-
Hats	-	-	-	-	-	+	-
Medicines	-	+	+	-	+	-	+
Mine props	-	+	+	+	+	-	-
Fish traps	-	-	-	-	+	+	+
Rail ties	-	-	+	+	+	-	-
Scaffolds	-	+	+	+	+	+	+
Tanning	-	+	+	-	+	-	-
Preservative	-	+	+	+	+	-	-
Timber	-	+	+	+	+	-	+
Tool handles	-	+	-	+	-	-	+
Fish smoking	+	+	-	-	-	-	-

by Semesi (1986). The commonly reported species of mangrove trees in coastal Tanzania are *Sonneratia alba, Rhizophora mucronata, Ceriops tagal, Bruguiera gymnorrhiza, Avicennia marina, Xylocarpus granatum, Heritiera littoralis* and *Lumnitzera racemosa. A. marina, R. mucronata* and *S. alba* are the most widespread species in Tanzania (McCusker, 1971).

Commercial and traditional products from the mangrove ecosystems are listed in Table 1 by species of mangrove. In India, leaves of *Avicennia* spp. are used as fodder for cattle and camels (Kukarni and Junagard, 1959). In Bangladesh, 177 t of honey and 49 t of beeswax are produced annually from *Execoecaria* spp., *Avicennia* spp. and other mangrove species (Macnae, 1974). Other products harvested in mangroves include crustaceans (prawns, lobsters and crabs), molluscs, and finfish (MacIntosh, 1983).

R. mucronata, B. gymnorrhiza, X. granatum, H. littoralis, S. alba, C. tagal, and *A. marina* face utilisation pressure in a decreasing order of intensity and resource management should respond to this intensity. In Tanzania, mangroves are used for firewood, charcoal, building poles and bark tannin (Mainoya, 1985) and *R. mucronata,* and *B. gymnorrhiza* are the most exploited species (Table 1). Attempts were made to introduce *R. mucronata* and *C. tagal* to the Rufiji Delta to replace the less useful *A. marina* and *S. alba* but it was not technically feasible.

The pioneer species *A. marina* colonises sandy-muddy sheltered areas and *S. alba* colonises muddy banks. Much of the literature supports the classic successional view of mangrove dynamics (Chapman, 1970, 1976) which explains zonation as a result of biotic processes which induce soil accumulation and plant community change from pioneer through to climax stage (Semesi, 1986). On the other hand, Thom (1982) suggested that mangrove patterns are ecological responses to external conditions of sedimentation, microtopography, estuarine hydrology and geochemistry. In order to understand the dynamics of mangrove distribution patterns, it is necessary to examine habitat change as a function of those processess which induce environmental change. This would in turn form the basis of a regeneration programme, for each species dominates the zone to which it is best adapted. In this respect, the Rufiji Delta forms a rare laboratory for regeneration studies of the mangroves. *Rhizophora mucronata,* the commonest species, is found either as extensive pure stands or in mixed vegetation. Within the main delta, the mangrove communities tend to be monospecific over appreciable areas, while mixed stands usually occur in the inner edge of mangroves (Semesi, 1986). Such zonations could easily be exploited for the successful regeneration of mangroves both in the delta and other parts of Tanzania.

Equally important in the management of mangroves is the organised exploitation of mature communities. Important felling and collection depots for poles and bark on the Rufiji Delta were Simba Ulanda, Dima, Urange, Mdae, Utikiti, Mohoro, Salale and Kikale. Others areas in Tanzania were Kisiju, Bagamoyo, Pangani, Mkindani, Idindi and Kilwa Masoko. In 1959, four cooperative societies were formed to take over the exploitation of mangroves in the Rufiji Delta. The societies operated under the umbrella of the Coast Region Co-operative Union Ltd. When cooperative unions were dissolved, disorganised harvesting, processing or marketing of mangrove products resulted despite significant local and export demand for poles. Reconstruction of organised systems for harvesting of mangroves is an important aspect of mangrove management programmes.

Open coasts

Tanzania's coastline extends 1,000 km from the Umba River in the north to the Ruvuma River in the south. The coastal zone is of varying width, 20 km to 70 km, gradually rising to a plateau.

Many wetlands of this formation have been modified by human activity, particularly rice cultivation. Coastal, riverine forests found in this area have a number of interesting plants, such as the endemic and monotypic genus of *Stuhlmannia* in the Pangani area. Flat sandy expanses on Mafia Island are dominated by *Philippia mafiensis* (Polhill, 1968). The fan palm (*Borassus aethiopium*) is also widespread. As its wood is resistant to termites, it is ideal for fencing posts and rafters; hollowed stems are sometimes used as water pipes, and fans, thatch, mats and baskets are made from its leaves. In central Tanzania, where this palm is also found, there are well established mat weaving activities supplying mats for clove drying in Zanzibar. The fruits are edible; root buds are used as vegetables and toddy is obtained from flowering stalks. *Borassus* is also used as an ornamental tree.

Wetlands in coastal forests

It is becoming increasingly clear that although evergreen and semi-green forests cover between 1-2% of Tanzania (887,000 km^2), these forests have a biological importance that is greater than their physical extent. This significance has been widely recognised for the 'Eastern Arc' montane forests, but many of the smaller forests of Tanzania are revealing remarkable biodiversity (Sheil and Burgess, 1990). In particular, the coastal forests have been highlighted as requiring further investigation (Lovett, 1985). There are 92 endemic trees in Tanzania's coastal forests (White, 1983). This high level of endemism is remarkable when compared with more extensive Tanzanian habitats. Coastal forests that attract considerable interest are Tanga limestone forests, GendaGenda Forest, Msungwe Forest, Kiono-Zaranginge Forest, Pande Forest, Pugu Hills forests, Kazimzubwi Forest, Vikindu Forest, Kisiju Forest, forests in the Rufiji Delta (Mchungu and Kikale), Ngarama and Pindiro forest reserves in Kilwa District, Rondo Forest; Chitoa, Ndiba, Ruawa, Matapwa, Litipo forest reserves in Lindi Region; Chilanga and Mahuta forest reserves in Mtwara Region; Jozani Forest in Zanzibar and the Ngezi forest reserve in Pemba.

The rare *Saintpaulia ionantha* (African Violet) has been found in abundance in the Kierengoma forest (Matumbi hills) (Johansson, 1978). This light sensitive species needs protection from unregulated logging operations in the riverine forest.

A study on nodulating legumes in the vicinity of Kierengoma (Sheil and Burgess, 1990) indicates some promising species which may lead to sustainable agroforestry systems. One variety of *Mimosa pudica* (sensitive plant) collected from a waterlogged area, showed abundant nodules on the roots and, more remarkably, on the stem (10-20 cm from the ground), suggesting that the plant may be adapted to nitrogen fixation in a waterlogged environment. If nitrogenase activity is confirmed in the stem nodules, then the potential for using such species in waterlogged environments, such as rice fields, could be investigated. The tree 'mtanga' (Caesalpinoidae) stimulates increased yields in the crops grown underneath it and could have potential use in more formalised cultivation systems. Discoveries of this kind demonstrate the practical value of coastal areas as a genetic resource (Sheil and Burgess, 1990).

Two hundred species of woody plants and herbs have been collected from the Pande and Zaraninge Forests for testing for anti-cancer activity by the National Cancer Institute in the USA (Burgess, 1990). Although these forests cover a total area of less than 250 km^2, their biological importance is such that they should be fully protected. Presently, all coastal forests are being threatened by unsustainable human actions including logging of canopy trees for timber and fuel; removal of hardwood poles to build houses; burning of woody plants to produce charcoal; and wholesale removal of woody vegetation for conversion of the land to agriculture. At the present rate of destruction, these remnant forest patches, with their globally important flora and fauna, could be decimated in the near future (Burgess, 1990).

Floodplains

Some floodplains occur in lowlands and terminate in estuarine deltas. Many of the larger rivers have floodplains which extend far inland with grassy marshes, flooded forests and ox-bow lakes. Floodplains are a conspicuous feature in the extensive Masai and Wembere Steppe, the Usangu Plains and the Rukwa and middle Malagarasi Basins. *Echinochloa pyramidalis* is characteristic of the main part of floodplains, with *Hyparrhenia rufa* found towards the margin; wooded areas are characterised by *Acacia* spp. or palm stands of *Hyphaene* and *Borassus* (Polhill, 1968).

Floodplains are mainly used for agriculture, notably rice cultivation. Clearing of land for agriculture and woodfuel is likely to lead to the removal of a number of plant species, in particular some *Acacia* species. *Trichilia emetica* is potentially an important soap industry tree in the Kyela and similar floodplains (Maro, 1984); *Khaya* spp. (mahogany) are important timber trees. In central Tanzania, *Tamarix* sp., a halophytic plant, forms part of the evergreen vegetation along the brackish Kigwe creek and floodplain. Such trees could be used to check soil salinisation and alkalinisation, a common feature of some irrigation projects, particularly in semi-arid environments (Nshubemuki, 1990).

Freshwater marshes

Freshwater marshes are common whenever groundwater, surface springs, streams or runoff cause frequent flooding or semi-permanent shallow water. Larger marshes, dominated by *Cyperus papyrus*, cattail (*Typha* spp.) and reed (*Phragmites*), with standing water most of the year are commonly termed swamps.

In Tanzania, freshwater swamps dominated by *C. papyrus* or *Phragmites* are extensive around Lakes Victoria and Tanganyika and also in scattered riverine localities, such as the middle reaches of the Malagarasi River (Usinge Swamps). Grassland swamp, with *Leersia* spp., *Pennisetum macrourum*, *Vossia cuspidata* and *Echinochloa stagnina* associated with Cyperaceae, is well developed in some of the interior drainage basins such as the Wembere, Bahi, Rukwa, Usangu and Usinge Swamps (Polhill, 1968).

Generally, most of the extensive swamps in Tanzania face no danger of destructive development, possibly because of the difficulties involved in reclamation.

Lakes

Lakes and ponds develop from several geomorphological processes including faulting, folding and stream action. Wave action and changes in seasonal water levels influence the kind of wetland vegetation that grows on lake and swamp margins. *Cyperus papyrus*, and occasionally *Phragmites*, typically form lake edge vegetation.

Woody vegetation associated with lakes includes *Vitex* spp., *Ficus* spp., *Albizzia* spp., *Cassia sangeuna* and *Sapium ellipticum*.

The surrounding vegetation traps runoff and stream flow, thus moderating the amount of nutrients and sediment that enters the lake. Such vegetation also forms important fish, bird and mammal habitats.

Peatlands

Under normal conditions, dead plant matter decomposes, eventually becoming carbon dioxide and water. Under conditions or low temperature, high acidity, low nutrient supply, waterlogging and oxygen deficiency, the decomposition process is retarded and dead plant matter accumulates as peat. Peatlands occur in all continents and latitudes, including the tropics where thick deposits can form in marshes and swamps, particularly in lake margins.

There is great diversity of peatlands worldwide, the pattern being governed by hydrology, acidity and climate. Some peatlands are highly acidic and nutrient-deficient, while others are neutral and nutrient-rich. Therefore, they include some of the least, as well as the most, productive wetlands.

In Tanzania, localised peatlands are found in the Southern Highlands, particularly Sao Hill (German Geological Mission in Tanzania, 1971), and in Ukinga (Geological Survey Department, 1958). Following a recent discovery of peatlands in Burundi, it is widely thought that parts of Kigoma Region, particularly the Kibondo and Kasulu Districts, could be extensions of the Burundi peatlands. Peat can be used as fuel and could alleviate the pressure on wood fuel. In addition, peatlands store carbon and they may have an important role as biogeochemical regulators, especially in relation to the Greenhouse Effect.

Swamp forests

Swamp forests develop in still water areas around lake margins, and in parts of floodplains, such as ox-bows, where water remains for long periods. Their precise character varies according to geographical location and environment.

In Tanzania, only semi-swamp forests occur. The Minziro Forest, which adjoins the Tanzania-Uganda border, is a semi-swamp forest covering 265 km^2. The forest has a variety of species usually found to the northwest or rarely found in other parts of Tanzania (e.g. *Heywoodia lucens, Podocarpus usambarensis var dawei, Mussaenda erythrophylla, Cassipourea ruwensorensis, Citropsis articulata, Manilkara obvata, Baikiaea insignis* and *Uncaria africana*).

Podocarpus spp. is commercially exploited and it is likely that the less marketable timber species found in this forest will gradually begin to be felled as *Podocarpus* stands dwindle.

The Jozani Forest in Zanzibar has the introduced oil palm (*Elaeis guineensis)* and *Pandanus*, as well as *Phoenix*, and *Anthocleista*. Another semi-swamp forest in Tanzania is found on Pemba Island; plant genera commonly found include *Chrysalidocarpus, Phoenix, Elaeis, Tabernaemontana*, and *Odyendea* (Polhill, 1986).

The semi-swamp forests in Zanzibar and Pemba have several rare and threatened species which could be conserved by translocation to nature reserves. Such species include *Ipomoea zanzibarica, Vanilla zanzibarica; Chrysalidocarpus pembanus* is the sole representative of this palm genus in East Africa; and *Typhodorum lindleyanum*, a native of Madagascar, occurs on Pemba (Polhill, 1968).

Phoenix reclinata, Ipomoea zanzibarica, and the wild yam (*Dioscorea*) can be used as disease resistant gene pools for genetic engineering of related cultivated species. *Vanilla zanzibarica* is of considerable interest to orchid collectors and for perfumery. Consumer demands are likely to require natural substances in consumer sensitive issues such as food and, to a lesser extent, perfumes.

Groundwater forests

The Rau Forest Reserve near Moshi is a groundwater forest. This Forest Reserve covers 25 km^2 and is of a lowland groundwater type. It contains a number of extremely interesting associates including *Oxystigma msoo* (Caesalpinioideae), unkown elsewhere and the only East African representative of a genus otherwise restricted to the Guinea-Congo forests. It is in association with *Milicia excelsa, Diospyros, Ficus, Lecaniodiscus, Acacia usambarensis* and *Tapura fischeri* (Polhill, 1968).

Much of this forest is no longer in its natural condition as timber is removed to supply poles and firewood to the adjoining Moshi townships. *Oxystigma msoo* trials were initiated at the Lushoto Silviculture Research Centre in the late 1970s.

The future of Tanzania's wetlands

The following functions are attributed to Tanzania's wetlands:

1. The wetlands on water catchments are involved in flood prevention, recharging ground water, controlling sedimentation and pollution and maintaining biodiversity.

2. Wetlands are important food sources (rice, sugar), breeding grounds for fish, wildlife and commercially important invertebrates.

3. A majority of landscape units serve as sources of forest products many of which lead to small scale industries such as soap making, carpentry, mat making, wine tapping.

4. They may be sources of plants useful for agroforestry and phytoreclamation, such as *Mimosa pudica*, 'Mtanga', and *Tamarix* sp.

5. Certain wetland vegetation types, such as the mangroves, are effective in the prevention of shore and beach erosion.

6. Wetlands are genetic warehouses; wild relatives of domesticated plants may be used in conferring resistance against disease.

The list is by no means exhaustive. Resource conservation in some of the wetlands needs improvement. Given the multi-utility perspective of wetlands and their diversity in structure, it is not possible to adopt a single conservation strategy. The only safeguard seems to be to prepare a list of uses and functions of wetlands and then let each use form the basis of a conservation programme. It is also important to solicit public goodwill in such programmes by conservation education through seminars and campaigns leading to public participation (Nshubemuki, 1990). What is advocated here is the ecosystem approach to conservation incorporating the preservation of genetic and ecological diversity with scientific research, environmental monitoring, education and training (di Castri and Robertson, 1982).

Most of the facets of Tanzania's flora and fauna have unique characteristics but these are not widely known by the Tanzanian community. Increasing public awareness of such characteristics needs to be strengthened so that this may guarantee their long term protection.

Bibliography

Banyikwa, F.F. 1986. The geographical distribution of mangrove forests along the East Africa coast. Pages 5-13. In: J.R. Mainoya and P.R. Siegel (Eds). *Status and Utilisations of Mangroves*. Proceedings of Workshop on 'Save the Mangrove Ecosystems in Tanzania'. 21- 22, February 1986. University of Dar es Salaam.

Botts, L. 1982. Swamps are important for people too. *Parks* 6(4):11-13.

Burgess, N.D. 1990. Preliminary results of the biological surveys in seven coastal forests of Tanzania: July - Sept. 1989. The society for Environmental Exploration (Frontier). Dar es Salaam/London.

Chapman, V.J. 1970. Mangrove phytosociology. *Trop. Ecol.* 11:1-19.

Chapman, V.J. 1976. *Mangrove vegetation.* J. Cramer, Vaduz. 447 pp.

Cohen, A. 1991. Patterns and controls of biodiversity within Lake Tanganyika. Paper Presented at 1st International Conference on the Conservation and Biodiversity of Lake Tanganyika. Faculty of Science, University of Burundi, Bujumbura.

Coulter, G. 1991. Management aspects of proposed underwater reserves in Lake Tanganyika. Paper Presented at 1st International Conference on the Conservation and Biodiversity of Lake Tanganyika. Faculty of Science, University of Burundi, Bujumbura.

di Castri, F. and J. Robertson. 1982. The Biosphere Reserve Concept: 10 years after. *Parks* 6(4):1-6.

Ford-Robertson, F.C. (Ed.). 1971. Terminology of Forest Science, Technology Practice and Products. The Multilingual Forestry Terminology Series No. 1. Society of American Foresters, Washington D.C. 12 pp.

Geological Survey Department. 1958. Quarter Degree Sheet 79 N.W. 1:125,000, Kipengere Geological Survey of Tanganyika, Dodoma.

German Geological Mission in Tanzania. 1971. Quarter Degree Sheet 232 1:125,000, Sao Hill. Geological Survey of the Federal Republic of Germany, Hannover.

Johansson, R.R. 1978. *Saintpaulias* in their natural environment. *Biological Conservation* 14:45-60.

Kukarni, D.H. and C.F. Junagard. 1959. Utilisation of mangrove forests in Saurashtra and Kutch. *Proc. Mangrove Symposium*, 1957, Calcutta. pp. 33-35.

Lovett, J.C. 1985. An overview of the moist forests in Tanzania. Tanzania National Scientific Research Council. Unpublished report.

Lowe-McConnell, R. 1991. Lake Tanganyika's unique fish fauna: Its importance in evolutionary studies and special opportunities it offers for biological research. Paper presented at 1st International Conference on the Conservation and Biodiversity of Lake Tanganyika. Faculty of Science, University of Burundi, Bujumbura.

MacIntosh, D.J. 1983. Wetlands of the world, riches lie in the tropical swamps. *Geographical Magazine* 19(4):184-188.

Macnae, W. 1974. Mangrove forests and fisheries. Indian Ocean Programme. No. 34, Indian Ocean Fishery Commission. 35 pp.

Mainoya, J.R. 1985. The distribution and socio-economic aspects of mangrove forests in Tanzania. Paper presented to a workshop on the socio-economic situation of pioneer settlement in mangrove forests Pattaya, Cholburi, Thailand, 27-31 May, 1985.

Maro, P.S. 1984. Vegetable oils in Tanzania: The availability of oilseeds for the soap industry. Report of phase III of the Geography sub-group. Dept. of Geography, University of Dar es Salaam. pp. 49-58.

McCusker, A. 1971. Ecological studies of an area of mangrove vegetation in Tanzania. Ph.D. thesis, University of Dar es Salaam.

Nshubemuki, L. 1990. Future needs and resources for research on natural forests in Tanzania: some views from TAFORI. Pages 168-170. In: I. Hedberg and E. Person (Eds). *Proceeding from a workshop on Research for Conservation of Tanzanian catchment Forests.* Morogoro, March 13-17, 1989.

Polhill, R.M. 1968. Tanzania. *Acta Phytogeographica Suecica* 54:166-178.

Semesi, A.K. 1986. Zonation and vegetation structure of mangrove communities in Tanzania. Pages 15-36. In: J.R Mainoya and P.R. Siegel (Eds). *Status and utilisation of Mangroves. Proceedings of workshop on 'Save the mangrove Ecosystems in Tanzania'. 21-22, February 1986.* University of Dar es Salaam.

Sheil, R.D. and N.D. Burgess. 1990. Preliminary results of biological surveys in Zaraninge (Kiono) and Kierengoma (Matumbi Hills) Coastal Forests, Tanzania Jan-March, 1990. Interim Report. The Society for Environmental Exploration (Frontier), Dar es Salaam/London.

Thom, B.G. 1982. Mangrove Ecology - A geomorphological perspective. Pages 3-17. In: B.F. Clough (Ed.) *Mangrove Ecosystems in Australia - Structure, Function and Management.* Australian Inst. of Mar. Sci.

White, F. 1983. Vegetation Map of Africa - A Description Memoir to Accompany the UNESCO/AETFAT/UNSO vegetation map of Africa. UNESCO, Paris.

The status of the fishery resource in the wetlands of Tanzania

P.O.J. Bwathondi and G.U.J. Mwamsojo

Tanzania Fisheries Research Institute
P.O. Box 9750
Dar es Salaam

Summary

The main types of wetlands in Tanzania are described as an introduction to a coverage of the fisheries of the large lakes, the minor waters, the rivers and the intertidal ecosystems. Fisheries potential is estimated and details of catches for each wetland type are given. Fishing techniques and the future of the fisheries are discussed and recommendations made for future wetlands fishery conservation.

Introduction

The term 'wetlands' includes a wide range of coastal and marine habitats, freshwater ponds, dams, swamps, rivers and lakes. The definition of wetlands provided by the Ramsar Convention (see Introduction) is used in this paper.

The freshwater fishery in Tanzania is divided into two main areas: the large bodies of water which include the Great Lakes (Victoria, Tanganyika and Nyasa), Lake Rukwa, Nyumba ya Mungu Dam and Mtera Dam; and the minor waters which include all small water bodies in Arusha, Dodoma, Iringa, Shinyanga, Singida, Tabora and Morogoro Regions and the Rufiji River.

The fishery of the deep Rift Valley lakes Tanganyika and Nyasa is concentrated in the pelagic zone offshore. In the other lakes the fishing is concentrated close to the shoreline, and in most cases, less than 20 m deep. Lake Rukwa, Mtera Dam and Nyumba ya Mungu Dam are very shallow (mean depth less than 5 m). In such shallow lakes the fishery is spread throughout the lake, with some concentration close to the shoreline. Fishing is very lucrative in the man made lakes (Nyumba ya Mungu Dam and Mtera Dam) and small inland lakes and swamps.

In the coastal zone, mangrove forests and estuarine ecosystems play a significant role in both finfish and shellfish fisheries. The major prawn fishing grounds are in Kisiju, Rufiji, Sadani and Bagamoyo (influenced by Ruvu and Wami Rivers). Prawns are harvested at a depth of between 1 m and 15 m. During high tides, prawn trawlers come to within a kilometre of the shore. Artisanal prawn fishermen, who drag their nets by hand, walk into shoulder-high water to set their nets.

Most fish use the estuarine ecosystem as nursery grounds for their young. The mangroves are nursery areas for prawns, crabs and fish, and settling sites for oysters. Studies on the mangrove crab (*Scylla serrata*) and the blue crab (*Portunus pelagicus*) have shown that these species have high potential in Tanzania.

General review of the wetlands of Tanzania

The major wetlands in Tanzania are shown in the Introduction to this volume. These include the major lakes Tanganyika, Nyasa and Victoria; the small lakes Rukwa, Manyara, Eyasi, Natron, Kitangiri, Burigi, Ikimba; and the rivers. There are many permanently flowing rivers whose catchments cover a wide area of the high altitudes of inland Tanzania. Table 1 shows the major drainage basins with their associated rivers and catchment areas. Most run through extensive basins which have either permanent marshes or are temporarily inundated by flood waters to form floodplains or swamps during the rainy season.

River Malagarasi, which flows westward into Lake Tanganyika, drains the Malagarasi swamp which is formed by the inland flowing Moyowosi and Gombe streams. The Katavi Swamp drains into Lake Rukwa through the Umba stream. Wembere Swamp is formed by Wembere and Manonga streams and is connected with Lake Eyasi through seasonal streams, forming a closed drainage system. Ugalla Swamp is drained by the Ugalla River, which joins the Wala stream to form the Sagara Swamp. Seasonal streams connect the Sagara Swamp to the Malagarasi River. Bahi Swamp has no outlet and is fed by the River Bubu.

Among the big rivers associated with extended basins is the River Ruaha, a major tributary of the River Rufiji, whose floodplains have deteriorated due to the construction of Mtera and Kidatu Dams. The Rufiji flows along a wide valley and has a delta covering 80,000 ha, the largest on the East African coast (Mbwana, 1986). Another major tributary is the River Kilombero, which floods annually and flows over a wide basin with small swamps and pools scattered throughout the length of the valley.

From Table 1, it can be seen that the majority (47%) of Tanzania drains into the Indian Ocean, 26% to interior drainage, 22% to the Atlantic ocean and 5% to the Mediterranean Sea. The importance of interior drainage and the associated fishery cannot be overemphasised.

Tanzania has a coastal zone which stretches for 800 km from 4°7'S in Tanga and 10°5'S in Mtwara Region (Banyikwa, 1986). Most rivers draining into the coastal zone originate in the highlands and flow to the Indian Ocean. The important rivers are shown in Table 1. At the entrance to the ocean, these rivers form an intertidal ecosystem, characterised by deltas and estuaries. Most of these deltas are covered by intertidal forests of mangrove trees.

Table 1   Major river systems and hydrological zones in Tanzania

Drainage basin	Major river systems	Catchment (1,000 km^2)	
Indian Ocean	Rufiji		177.4
	Ruvuma		52.1
	Wami		46.4
	Pangani and others		42.1
	Matandu		18.6
	Ruvu		18.4
	Mbwemkuru		16.3
	Lake Nyasa-Ruhuhu		14.0
	Mbezi and others		7.7
	Umba		6.7
	Lukuledi		6.0
	Others		32.4
		Total	438.1
Interior Drainage	Rift Valley rivers		64.5
	Lake Eyasi and Kitangiri		64.4
	Babu River		25.6
	Masai Steppes		10.9
	Others		78.7
		Total	244.1
Atlantic Ocean (Lake Tanganyika)	Malagarasi		126.1
	Luiche		2.6
	Others		80.3
		Total	209.0
Mediterranean Sea (Lake Victoria)	Grumeti		11.7
	Simiyu		11.6
	Mblageti		5.7
	Mirare/Mori		0.8
	Mara		0.8
	Others		21.3
		Total	50.3

Table 2   The distribution of mangrove swamps in Tanzania (Source: Mbwana, 1986; Banyikwa, 1986)

Zone	Area covered (ha)		Per cent coverage %
Tanga Region			
Tanga District		10,004	
Pangani District		600	
	Total	10,604	10.8
Coast Region			
Rufiji District		40,500	
Bagamoyo District		1,501	
Kisarawe District		3,501	
Mafia District		405	
	Total	45,907	46.7
Lindi Region			
Kilwa District		14,005	
Lindi District		1,418	
	Total	15,423	15.7
Mtwara Region		8,003	8.2
Pemba Island		12,000	12.3
Zanzibar Island		6,000	6.1
TOTAL		**97,937**	**99.8**

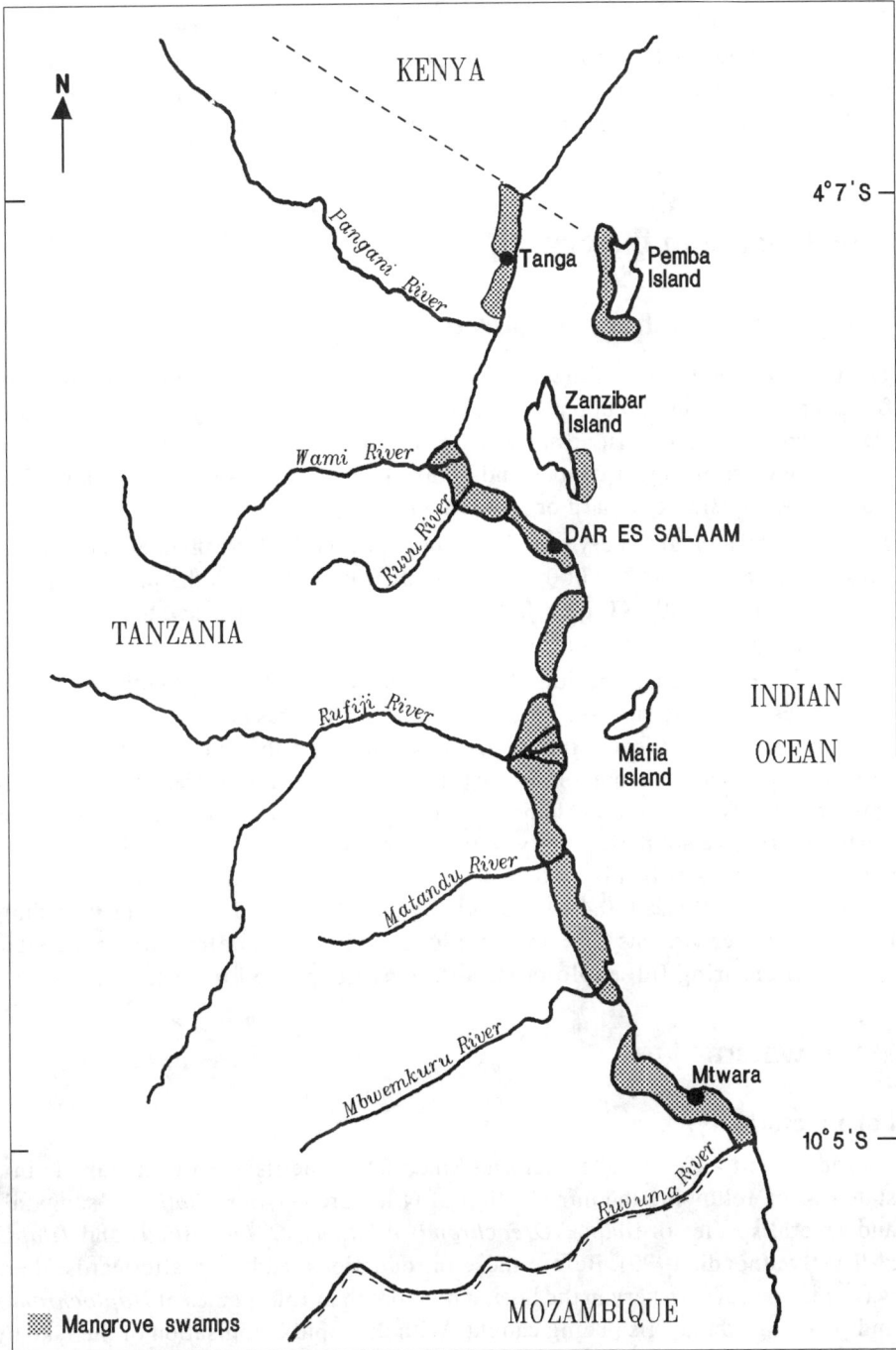

Figure 1   Mangrove swamps along the Tanzanian coast

Table 2 and Figure 1 show the distribution and area of mangrove forests in Tanzania; the Rufiji Delta contains 41.4% of Tanzania's mangroves.

Outside the intertidal zone is the seagrass bed area which also acts as the nursery ground for many juvenile, coastal fish, especially herbivores. It is in this area that the artisanal fishery, using mainly beach seines, is concentrated.

The Tanzanian fishery

The potential fishery resource

The fishing population in Tanzania is estimated to be 64,241 permanent, full-time fishermen and about 300,000 part-time fishermen. The majority use simple equipment such as gill nets, cast nets, traps, hooks and seine nets. Simple crafts, dugout canoes, dhows, outrigger canoes and planked canoes are used as well as modern wooden boats using outboard or inboard engines.

The potential, annual fishery production in Tanzania (both freshwater and marine) is estimated to be over 730,000 t (Bwathondi, 1990) although the present catches are less than 400,000 t (Tables 3, 4 and 5). Catches from freshwater account for more than 87.5% of total fish catches.

Current *per capita* consumption of fish in Tanzania is 13.5 kg (Bwathondi, 1990) which is estimated to rise to 20 kg by the year 2000. This can only be achieved if more investment is injected into the fishery and less fish are exported. However, research and fisheries reports indicate that some artisanal fisheries are either fully exploited or over-exploited, hence the expected catches may not be achieved unless alternative sources, mainly in the inland waters, are identified. The major source of freshwater fish is Lake Victoria (54.2%) followed by Lake Tanganyika (31%) and Lake Nyasa (10.4%). Reports by Bwathondi and Mahika (1989) show that deep water prawns are underexploited whereas shallow water penaeid prawns are nearing full exploitation or are overexploited in certain areas.

Major waters

Lake Victoria

Tanzania owns 47% of Lake Victoria. Since 1960, the fishery of this lake is in a state of flux following the introduction of Nile Perch (*Lates niloticus*, 'sangara') and several species of tilapia (*Oreochromis niloticus, O. leucosticus* and *Tilapia zillii*) (Bwathondi, 1990). Before these introductions, and soon afterwards, there was a multispecies fishery in the lake, with more than 150 species of *Haplochromis* and several genera of fish being caught. With the rapid colonisation of the lake by *L. niloticus*, the fishery has been reduced to a few important species. By the end of 1990, only were considered economically important, *L. niloticus*, the tilapias (mainly *O. niloticus*, 'sato') and *Rastrineobola argentea* ('dagaa') were considered economically important.

Most fish in Lake Victoria are captured by the simple fishing gear mentioned in the previous section. Gill nets, generally 4" to 5" mesh, are set in deeper waters of less than 20 m. Some fishermen set the nets in the evening, leave them overnight and haul them in the next morning, while others leave them permanently in the water and inspect them every morning (Bwathondi, 1991).

Beach seine nets are popular along the sandy shore of the lake. The net is set in less than 5 m of water and hauled in within a few hours. Catches include adults and juveniles of most shallow water species. There are large seine nets whose operations take up to 8 hours from setting to retrieving.

Traps are usually set in rivers, marshes and close to the shoreline. Those set in the rivers and marshes capture riverine fish which spawn in the rivers but grow and feed in the lake (potamodromous fish) or those which spawn in the lake but feed in rivers (Bwathondi *et al.*, 1991). The most common genera found in the rivers and marshes of Lake Victoria include *Labeo*, *Schilbe* and *Protopterus*. The capture of these fish, especially at breeding time during the rainy season, has contributed substantially to their decline in the lake.

Besides the large piscivorous fish of Lake Victoria (*Lates*, *Bagrus* and *Clarias*) and the riverine fish mentioned above, there is a growing fishery of freshwater sardines ('dagaa') in Lake Victoria. The 'dagaa' are pelagic and are caught with a purse seine or lift net using light attraction.

The fishery of Lake Victoria has grown rapidly from 72,600 t in 1983 to over 200,000 t from 1986 onwards and accounts for 54.2% of the total catch from major lakes (see Table 3).

Table 3   Annual fish production from major freshwater wetlands in Tanzania
(1983-1989)

Wetland	1983	1984	1985	1986	1987	1988	1989	%
	thousand tonnes							
Lake Victoria	72.6	99.7	100.8	217.2	159.9	205.5	207.5	54.2
Lake Tanganyika	99.4	107.1	115.2	70.0	93.7	62.7	53.5	31.0
Lake Nyasa	19.5	18.1	27.0	35.9	30.0	39.3	34.5	10.4
Lake Rukwa	4.8	4.6	4.6	5.9	8.1	5.8	8.9	2.2
Nyumba ya Mungu Dam	3.4	1.8	1.8	2.0	2.0	5.0	3.9	1.0
Mtera Dam	2.4	3.6	2.4	3.3	3.4	3.8	4.3	1.2
Total	202.1	234.9	251.8	334.3	297.1	322.1	312.6	100

Lake Tanganyika

Tanzania owns 45% of Lake Tanganyika. The fish stocks of Lake Tanganyika consist mainly of pelagic species such as *Stolothrissa tanganicae, Limnothrissa miodon* and the predators, *Lates* spp. No current estimates are available for potential yield but it is known that the Tanzanian part of the lake is less productive than either the Burundian or Zambian parts, where both artisanal and commercial fisheries are well developed and the sustainable catches are estimated to be 116 kg/ha and 140 kg/ha respectively.

The commercial fishery is localised within a small area of the Kigoma waters and reflects symptoms of local overfishing. This fishery is adversely affected by continuously falling levels of the total catch from 100,000 t in 1983 to 60,000 t in 1989 (see Table 3). There have been prolonged low levels in abundance of *Stolothrissa tanganicae* accompanied by damping of catch oscillations during the last twelve years. The abundance of *Limnothrissa miodon*, an inshore species, has increased in offshore waters, negatively correlated with oscillations of its predator, *Lates mariae*.

Fishing in Lake Tanganyika is carried out by scoop netting and gill netting using light attraction. Gill nets and traps are deployed in the rivers draining into the lake, especially the Malagarasi system. The importance of the Malagarasi River system, including swamps, on the fishery of the lake cannot be overemphasised. The decline of the lake species could be related to the productivity of fish species in the Malagarasi River.

A project funded through FAO and FINIDA will investigate the productivity of Lake Tanganyika, with a view to advising on the development of fisheries in the lake.

Lake Nyasa

Lake Nyasa is shared by Tanzania, Malawi and Mozambique and has a diverse fish fauna. The main genera found in the Tanzanian side are Oreochromis ('perege'), Haplochromis ('utapi'), Engraulicypris ('dagaa'), Rhamphochromis ('ngerewa'), Clarias ('kambale'), Bagrus ('kitoga'), Opsaridion ('mbasa'), Synodontis ('ngogo') and Labeo ('ningu'). Bioproductivity is generally low on the Tanzania side due to the steepness of the shore. The main fishing crafts, dugout canoes, can operate over short distances offshore using gill nets, chilimila nets and long lines. Annual fish production increased from 19,500 t in 1983 to 39,300 t in 1988 (Table 3).

Lake Rukwa

A shallow lake, Lake Rukwa is surrounded by a highly vegetated fringe which supports a productive fishery. The most important fish are *Oreochromis* spp., *Clarias gariepinus* and *Bagrus* spp., caught from dugout canoes with gill nets and long lines. Fish productivity has increased as a result of the rise in the level of the lake and an increase in vegetation around the margins.

Mtera Dam

Mtera Dam was completed in 1982 on the River Ruaha, changing the riverine system into a lacustrine environment. The population of fish increased quickly due to plentiful food provided by decomposing plant material and submerged vegetation. The dam was colonised by genera which were found in the River Ruaha, including *Oreochromis*, *Clarias*, *Synodontis*, *Schilbe*, *Labeo*, *Alestes* and *Hydrocyon*. Annual fish catches have almost doubled from 2,400 t in 1983 to 4,300 t in 1989 (Table 3). Fish are caught with gill nets and long lines from dugout canoes. Recently the population of fishermen has increased rapidly and must be controlled to avoid overfishing in the dam.

Nyumba ya Mungu Dam

Nyumba ya Mungu Dam is a multipurpose impoundment covering 18,000 ha. Construction was completed in 1965 to store water for hydropower generation on the Pangani River. Soon after its construction, the fish population in the dam increased and attracted many fishermen. The resulting fishing pressure has caused overfishing of tilapia, the major fish stock.

Minor Waters

A total of 10,500 t of fish were caught in minor waters in 1989 (Table 4). Singida, Arusha and Dodoma Regions produced 35.6%, 23.5% and 18.6% of fish from minor waters respectively. The fishery resource in minor waters consists mainly of riverine genera, such as *Oreochromis* and *Clarias*, which are caught from dugout canoes with traps, hooks, gill nets, weirs and occasionally beach seines. In floodplains, fishing is carried out during the rainy season and in pools which become isolated as the river levels drop. In such pools, fish are caught with basket traps and spears.

Although fishing activities may take place all year round, the most important fishing period is during the rainy season, as at this time fish ascend the rivers to spawn and are easy prey.

The River Rufiji plays an important role in the riverine fishery of Tanzania. Most fishing activities are carried out in the major tributaries, the Ruaha and Kilombero Rivers. However, fishing activities in parts of River Ruaha, the largest tributary of River Rufiji, have been reduced by construction of Mtera and Kidatu dams, which control the floods. The Kilombero River contributes considerably to the *Clarias*, *Distichodus*, *Bagrus* and tilapia fisheries.

The catch from the minor waters is summarised in Table 4. In the Dodoma Region, the major contributors of fish are the Bahi Swamp and the Hombole Dam; the latter is important for the production of fingerlings for aquaculture projects in the region.

Lake Kitangiri contributes 60% to the total production of the Singida Region and future fishery development and planning should be focussed on this lake.

The new Sola Dam and Mhumbi Dam contribute more than 50% to the total catch of the Shinyanga Region.

Table 4   Annual fish production from minor freshwater wetlands in Tanzania
(1983-1989)

Region	1983	1984	1985	1986	1987	1988	1989	%
	thousand tonnes							
Arusha	0.18	0.18	3.64	0.10	1.00	4.30	1.10	23.5
Dodoma	1.80	0.69	0.25	0.66	1.31	2.22	1.40	18.6
Singida	1.53	2.04	0.98	2.18	2.14	2.20	4.90	35.6
Shinyanga	-	0.03	0.03	0.02	0.03	0.03	0.03	0.4
Tabora	0.11	0.18	1.04	0.36	0.36	0.68	0.22	6.6
Iringa	-	-	-	-	0.06	-	0.16	0.5
Morogoro	-	-	0.02	0.91	0.69	-	2.18	8.5
Coast	-	-	2.02	-	0.35	-	0.52	6.3
Total	3.62	3.12	7.98	4.23	5.94	9.43	10.51	100

Table 5   Annual fish production from marine wetlands in Tanzania (1983-1989)

Region	1983	1984	1985	1986	1987	1988	1989	%
	thousand tonnes							
Tanga	6.02	6.22	4.55	4.40	4.86	7.62	5.44	13.6
Coast	11.95	11.46	10.74	10.75	11.40	11.95	11.00	27.4
Dar es Salaam	5.31	4.81	6.84	10.66	6.35	14.00	15.26	21.9
Lindi	6.13	9.80	11.59	14.05	7.05	5.97	8.04	21.8
Mtwara	3.97	7.50	7.96	5.33	7.33	5.33	7.41	15.3
Total	33.38	39.79	41.68	45.19	36.99	44.87	47.15	100

The Ugalla River complex contributes substantially to fish production in the Tabora Region. Attention should be paid to fishery development in the Mbona and Shela waters.

Near the mouth of the Rufiji River there is an important fishery for estuarine fish. The file fish *(Amanses)*, milkfish *(Chanos chanos)* and catfish *(Arias)* are caught within the delta and in the coastal waters of the Rufiji River system.

Intertidal waters

Table 5 summarises the fish production in marine waters in Tanzania, which accounts for only 12.6% of the total fish production in Tanzania. The Coast Region contributes more than any other region (27.4%) to total marine landings. The high figure for Dar es Salaam is partly due to landings at both Banda and Kunduchi beaches of fish from Mafia, Bagamoyo and Zanzibar. Some of these fish may have been recorded first in their respective fishing districts and again in Dar es Salaam.

The major landings of the coast include the groupers, catfish, sardines, rabbitfish, sharks, lobsters and prawns. Important wetland habitats include the mangrove swamps and estuaries. Mangrove areas are rich in organic material due to foliage drop and decay. Alluvium, which is rich in both organic and inorganic nutrients, is deposited by the incoming river. The common fish found in the mangrove and estuarine habitats include milkfish, catfish and file fish; several prawn species use mangroves as nursery areas.

There are more than 30 species of prawns in Tanzanian waters but the economically important ones include *Penaeus monodon*, *P. indicus*, *P. semisulcatus* and *P. latisulcatus*. The largest, and most valuable prawn is *P. monodon*, whereas *P. indicus* is the most abundant in Tanzanian waters.

Presently there are more than 10 trawlers fishing for prawns in Tanzania. As well as prawns, these trawlers also catch fish (by-catch) which can account for up to 70% of the total catch. Because of the limited storage space on board most trawlers, the fish are often discarded. TAFIRI (Tanzania Fisheries Research Institute), in collaboration with experts from NORAD, is designing a method to separate prawns from fish and reduce by-catch waste.

Seagrass beds are nursery and feeding grounds for herbivorous fish, such as parrotfish *(Scarus)*, rabbitfish *(Siganus)* and as habitats for *Bech-de-mer* and the bivalves *Anadara antiquata*. Men usually catch fish using seine nets, while *A. antiquata* and *Bech-de-mer* are hand picked by women. This type of fishery is very prominent in areas close to Dar es Salaam and the mudflats of Ocean Road, Kaole and Mjimwema beaches, and around Zanzibar, Mafia and Pemba Islands.

Recommendations

It is recommended that the swamps, especially in the Malagarasi River and the hinterland drainage system, should be conserved and not used for rice growing, as they are a major source of freshwater fish.

As several diverse user groups are involved in the utilisation of man-made lakes and dams, management of these areas should be under one administration which could cater for the interests of the different groups.

More research should be carried out on the fish fauna and ecology of wetlands.

Studies on the control of the Water Hyacinth, which is becoming a threat to Lake Victoria and its fisheries, should be carried out with the assistance of donor agencies.

Bibliography

Banyikwa, F.F. 1986. The geographical distribution of mangrove forests along the East African Coast. Pages 5-13. In: J.E. Mainoya and P.R. Siegel (Eds). *Status and Utilization of Mangroves. Proceedings of a workshop on 'Save the Mangrove Ecosystems in Tanzania'*, 21-22 February 1986. University of Dar es Salaam.

Bwathondi, P.O.J. 1990. The state of fishing industry in Tanzania with particular reference to inland fishery. *Proceedings of a Seminar on Prevailing Activities on the Lake Victoria Basin with Particular Reference to the Fisheries of the Lake*, 8-9 March 1990. Mwanza, Tanzania. pp. 5-11.

Bwathondi, P.O.J. 1991. The fisheries resources of Lake Victoria. Paper presented to the National Seminar on the Fisheries of Lake Victoria, October 1991. Mwanza.

Bwathondi, P.O.J., J.J. Kulekana and G.U.J. Mwamsojo. 1991. Survey and monitoring of the fishery of Mindu Dam and man made lake in Morogoro, Tanzania. Unpublished report. 51 pp.

Bwathondi, P.O.J. and G.C. Mahika. 1989. Prawn fishery of Tanzania based on data from TAFICO (1983-1988). Unpublished report. 21 pp.

Mbwana, S.B. 1986. Mangrove conservation and utilization in Tanzania. Pages 46-69. In: J.E. Mainoya and P.R. Siegel (Eds). *Status and Utilization of mangroves. Proceedings of a workshop on 'Save the Mangrove Ecosystems in Tanzania'*, 21-22nd February 1986. University of Dar es Salaam.

Wildlife resources and tourism in wetlands of Tanzania

E.B. Mpemba

Wildlife Division
P.O. Box 1994
Dar es Salaam

Summary

The presence of wetlands in the various protected areas in Tanzania (national parks, game reserves, controlled areas and the Ngorongoro Special Conservation Area) is described. The value of tourism in wetlands and the problems of wildlife in wetlands is discussed. Recommendations for the management of wetlands in reserves emphasises the necessary involvement of people who live adjacent to these areas and are affected by management decisions.

Introduction

The reserved areas in Tanzania are summarised in Table 1. In Table 2 the conservation status of large freshwater wetlands of the Zaire River drainage and Lakes Tanganyika, Nyasa, and Victoria are shown. Table 3 shows the wetlands of the eastern Rift Valley and the eastern drainage system.

There are 56 controlled areas where wildlife exists alongside human activities such as farming and fishing.

Laws governing wetlands

If a wetland is within a national park or game reserve, then its management falls under the control of the Director of Wildlife. Hydropower dams are controlled by the Tanzanian Electricity Company (TANESCO). In some areas, for example the Bahi Swamps, the wildlife is under the control of the Director of Wildlife but the wetland is managed by the villagers.

Table 1 Protected areas of Tanzania and their status, with reference to wetland conservation

Protected areas	Area (km²)	Wetland system	Features of significance
National parks			
Arusha	137	Riverine, lacustrine, palustrine	Ngurudoto Crater, watershed for Pangani system
Katavi	2,253	Riverine, palustrine	Rukuru, Katavi Swamp system
Kilimanjaro	756	Riverine, palustrine	Watershed
Lake Manyara	320	Lacustrine, palustrine, riverine	Lake Manyara
Mikumi	3,230	Riverine, palustrine	Ruvu, Wami and Ruaha watersheds
Ruaha	12,950	Riverine, palustrine	Usangu plain, Ruaha watershed
Rubondo	457	Lacustrine	Lake Victoria shore
Serengeti	14,763	Riverine, palustrine, lacustrine	Watershed to part of Lake Victoria
Tarangire	2, 600	Riverine, palustrine	Tarangire Swamp
Game reserves			
Biharamulo	1,300	Lacustrine, riverine	Lake Victoria shore
Burigi	2,200	Lacustrine, riverine	Lake Burigi
Ibanda	200	Riverine, lacustrine	Lake Twamwala and Kagera River
Kizigo	4,000	Riverine, palustrine	Ruaha watershed
Maswa	2,200	Riverine	Lake Eyasi and Wembere watershed
Mkomazi	1,000	Riverine	Pangani watershed
Moyowosi	6,000	Riverine	Moyowosi watershed
Rumanyika	800	Riverine	Kagera watershed
Rungwa	9,000	Riverine, palustrine	Rungwa and Ruaha watersheds
Sadani	300	Marine, estuarine	Marine and estuarine habitats
Selous	50,000	Palustrine, riverine	Rufiji floodplain, Rufiji watershed
Ugalla	5,000	Riverine	Malagarasi-Moyowosi system
Uwanda	5,000	Lacustrine, riverine	Lake Rukwa system
Conservation areas			
Ngorongoro	8,288	Riverine, lacustrine	Lake Magadi, watersheds for Lakes Eyasi, Manyara and Natron

Table 2   Large feshwater wetlands associated with the Zaire River, and Lakes
Tanganyika, Nyasa and Victoria; their status and special features
(Source: Chabwela, 1991)

Name	Wetland types	Approx. size (km^2)	Conservation status	Special features
Rukwa	Shallow lake	2,300	Partially protected as controlled area and game reserve	Wildlife, grazing and fishery
Malagarasi	Floodplain and swamp	7,360	Partially protected as game reserve and controlled area	Wildlife, grazing and fishery
Moyowosi	Swamp and floodplain	-	Partially protected and controlled area	Wildlife
Lake Tanganyika	Swamp, shore	-	Uncontrolled	Fishery
Lake Nyasa	Swamp, shore	-	Unprotected	Fishery, agriculture and grazing
Lake Burigi	Shallow lake	-	Unprotected	Fishery, agriculture and grazing
Upper Kagera	Shallow lake	350	Partly protected as controlled area	Wildlife, agriculture and grazing
Lake Ikimba	Shallow lake	-	Unprotected	Fishery and agriculture
Lake Victoria	Swamp, shore	-	Largely unprotected	Fishery, agriculture and grazing
Mara River system	Swamp and floodplain	30,000	Unprotected	Agriculture, fishery and grazing

Table 3   Large wetlands of the East Rift Valley and the eastern hydrological
systems; their status and special features (Source: Chabwela, 1991;
IUCN/WWF/NEMC, 1990)

Name	Wetland types	Conservation status	Special features
Usangu	Floodplain, swamp (520 km^2)	Partially protected as controlled area	Wildlife, grazing, agriculture
Kilombero	Floodplain, swamp (6,650 km^2)	Partially protected as controlled area	Fishery, wildlife, grazing, agriculture
Rufiji	Floodplain (1,450 km^2)	Partially protected as game reserve	Agriculture, wildlife, fishery
Liwale	Swamp	Unprotected	Fishery, agriculture
Ruvu River system	Floodplain, swamp (43,000 km^2)	Partially protected as controlled area	Fishery, grazing, agriculture
Mkata-Tendigo	Floodplain and swamp	Unprotected	Fishery, grazing, agriculture
Bahi Swamp	Swamp (125,000 km^2)	Unprotected	Fishery, wildlife, grazing
Pangani system	Swamp, floodplain (90,000 km^2)	Fully protected as controlled area	Agriculture, fishery, grazing
Olgarwa-Shambari	Swamp	Fully protected as controlled area	Agriculture, fishery, grazing
Ngusero	Swamp	Protected as controlled area	Agriculture, grazing, wildlife
Tarangire	Swamp (60,000 km^2)	Protected as part of a National Park	Wildlife
Lake Manyara	Shallow sodic lake, swamp (41,300 km^2)	Partially protected as National Park and controlled area	Wildlife, grazing, agriculture
Lake Natron	Shallow sodic lake (85,500 km^2)	Protected as controlled area	Grazing, wildlife
Lake Balangida	Shallow sodic lake (6,000 km^2)	Unprotected	Agriculture, grazing
Lake Balangida Lelu	Shallow sodic lake (3,000 km^2)	Unprotected	Agriculture, grazing
Ngorongoro Crater	Shallow lake	Protected as conservation area	Wildlife, grazing
Lake Eyasi	Seasonal shallow sodic lake (116,000 km^2)	Partially protected as controlled area	Agriculture, fishery, wildlife
Wembere	Floodplain, swamp	Unprotected	Wildlife, agriculture, fishery, grazing
Lake Kitangiri	Shallow lake	Unprotected	Fishery, agriculture
Wami River	Estuarine	Unprotected	Fishery, agriculture
Rufiji Delta	Estuarine	Unprotected	Fishery, wildlife, agriculture

Wildlife in wetlands

Animals tend to congregate around wetlands. There are some species which are always found near water, such as hippopotamus, waterbuck, warthog, elephant, crocodile, sitatunga, and waterbirds such as flamingos and ducks. These animals are part of a complex food chain which is reflected in the high diversity of biota in wetlands.

Economic value of wildlife in wetlands

Wetlands provide people with a source of food and skins. Local people hunt for food while the tourist from abroad hunts for trophies, such as skins, horns and ivory. In some areas, illegal hunting has caused wildlife numbers to decline and the Government of Tanzania has neither the finance nor the manpower to control it. The international community has provided funds to assist Tanzania to manage its wildlife. Also, NGOs such as the World Wildlife Fund (WWF), the African Wildlife Fund (AWF), the World Conservation Union (IUCN), German Technical Assistance, YOU Magazine and individuals have been involved in wildlife conservation and management in Tanzania.

Tourism

Tourism is the major activity in wetlands where there is a high concentration of wildlife. It is impossible to develop infrastructures in all wetlands of Tanzania because many are very remote. The Bahi Swamps, in Dodoma Region, and Lake Kitangiri, in Singida Region, are well known for their bird life but the long and rough road from Dodoma to these places precludes any tourist development there. Perhaps future generations will develop these areas and use them for recreation.

If these areas can be developed then tourism has the potential to become a major foreign exchange earner in Tanzania.

Human-wildlife interactions in wetlands

The major problem in wetlands is poaching for both meat and ivory. The wildlife resource is threatened by the greed and short term views of the poachers and their masters.

There is a conflict of interest between the conservators of wildlife and farmers. When wild animals destroy crops, property and livestock no compensation is paid to the farmers. This has resulted in the farming community resenting the presence of wildlife. In some areas, there is competition between livestock and wildlife for grazing areas; villagers in Mkomazi and Ugalla want the game reserves to be available for livestock grazing.

No traditional fishing and honey collecting is allowed in national parks and game reserves. People resent this as they receive no tangible benefits from the presence of these protected areas in their vicinity.

Recommendations

The Wildlife Division of the Ministry of Tourism Natural Resources and Environment should work closely with villagers who live near the wetlands so that they are involved in the management of the wetland and can see the value of conservation.

The government should create a wetland authority which will be responsible for planning the management of wetlands for the whole country.

Since the government owns the wildlife and receives monetary benefit from its existence, it should compensate villagers for damage done to property, crops and livestock.

Legislation governing the conservation of wetlands should be made more relevant to current needs.

International bodies should be approached to assist Tanzania in the development of remote wetland areas, such as Wembere, Malagarasi, Lake Kitangiri and Bahi Swamps.

Bibliography

NEMC/WWF/IUCN. 1990. *Development of a Wetland Conservation and Management Programme for Tanzania.* IUCN, Switzerland. 113 pp.

Chabwela, H. 1991. Tanzania. Southern Africa Wetlands Programme, Draft Report. Chapter 9. IUCN, Harare, Zimbabwe.

Water supply from wetlands in Tanzania

J.M. Mihayo

Ministry of Water, Energy and Minerals
P.O. Box 350666
Dar es Salaam

Summary

This paper gives a brief discussion on water supply from wetlands in Tanzania. The major drainage basins in Tanzania are described and the status and role of the Division of Water Research in the monitoring of water resources and data collection from wetlands and water sources are highlighted. The role of wetlands in the hydrological cycle, and the utilisation of wetlands as water supply sources are discussed. The need for conservation and protection of wetlands and other water sources is outlined.

Introduction

The definition of wetlands used in this paper follows that of the Ramsar Convention and is found in the Introduction to this volume.

Figure 1 shows that Tanzania is divided into five major drainage basins, classified according to the recipient of the water: the Indian Ocean (Pangani, Wami, Ruvu, Rufiji and Ruvuma Rivers, and Lake Nyasa); internal drainage to Lake Eyasi and Bubu depression complex; internal drainage to Lake Rukwa; drainage to the Atlantic Ocean; and drainage to the Mediterranean Sea (*via* Lake Victoria). Each of these basins includes a network of rivers, lakes and wetlands.

The Division of Water Research, in the Ministry of Water, Energy and Minerals, is responsible for monitoring of all the water resources in Tanzania, both surface and underground. In addition to water resource monitoring, the Division provides the necessary hydrological and hydrogeological expertise to facilitate the design of new water development projects and expansion of the existing schemes such as dams, water supply systems, hydropower development and flood control. The Division is the custodian of the national hydrological and hydrogeological data banks.

In 1971, the government launched a 20 year water supply programme with the primary objective that, by the year 1991, the majority of people would have access

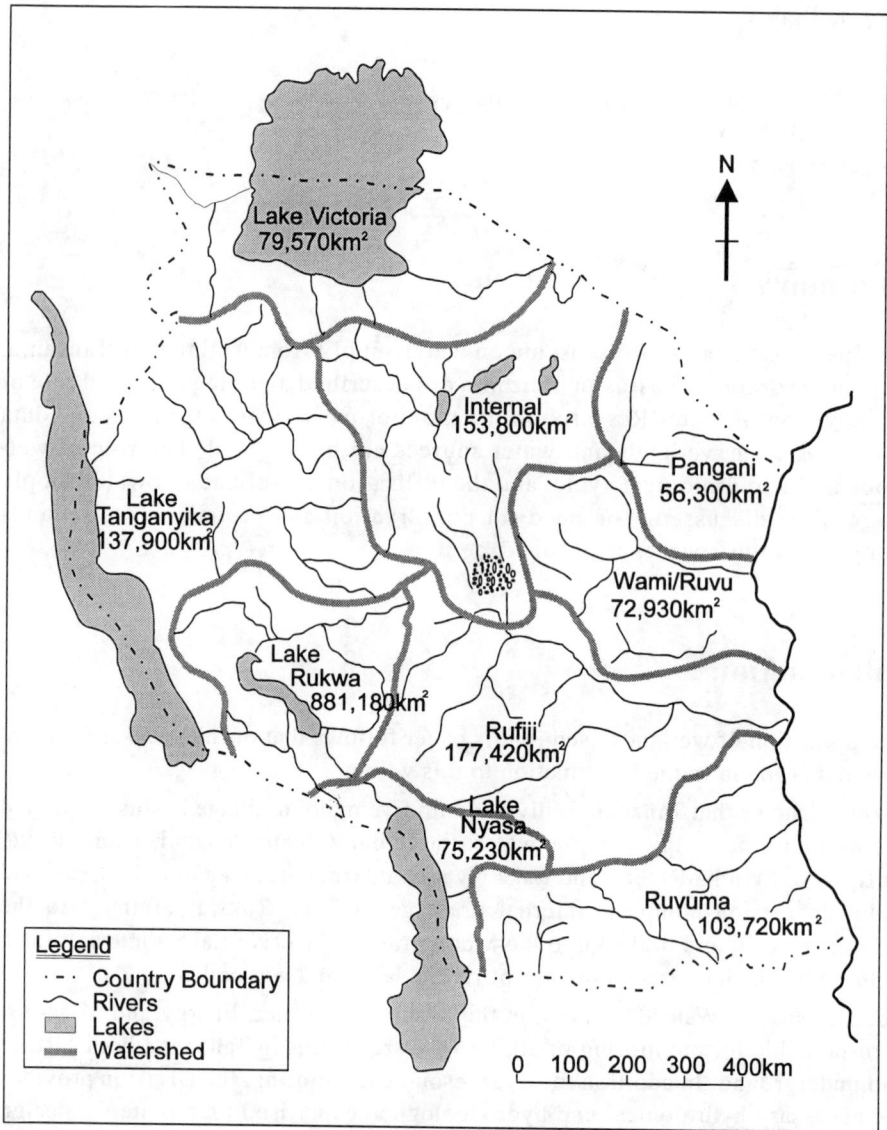

Figure 1   Major drainage basins of Tanzania showing catchment areas in km²

to clean and safe water within 400 m of each household. However, due to financial and other constraints, the planned programmes have had a slow rate of implementation and the government now intends that this goal be attained by the year 2002.

Due to the importance of water resource data in the design of projects, several Regional Water Master Plans were initiated by the government in the 1970s. The objective of the plans was to determine Tanzania's water resources, now and in the future. The Division of Water Research was a major participant in the Water Master Plans through its three sections, hydrology, hydrogeology and drilling.

The Ministry of Water, Energy and Minerals has the responsibility for policy development, preparation of long term plans, construction of regional projects, and execution of all national water projects. The Division of Water Research is responsible for the operation and maintenance of the hydrometric network of stations which are scattered all over the country. At these stations, the quantity and the quality of the water sources are determined and the data is used in the design of water development and related projects.

Hydrometric, rainfall and climatological stations have been established to monitor major water bodies, rainfall and climate. Today, the Division operates 351 hydrometric, 348 rainfall and 89 climatological stations. Wetlands, such as rivers, springs, lakes and reservoirs are covered in the network.

In addition to the rivers, the Division also monitors water level fluctuations in reservoirs, dams and 'charcos' which are, in addition to groundwater, the major sources of water for the arid and semi-arid Regions of Singida, Dodoma, Shinyanga and Tabora. Dams and 'charcos' are widely used in these semi-arid areas of Tanzania for people as well as livestock. Table 1 shows the distribution and uses of dams in Tanzania.

Some reservoirs in the country are in danger of losing their storage capacity, due mainly to the high rate of sedimentation. Many of these reservoirs and dams have never been surveyed to determine actual storage capacity. In this regard, it is difficult to make rational decisions on the utilisation of the water since the available quantity is not known precisely.

Industrial pollution of rivers has occurred in Tanga Region where some sisal estates discharge untreated effluents directly into the rivers, thereby depleting the dissolved oxygen in the water. Another common source of pollution is caused by livestock fouling human water sources.

Hydrology of wetlands

Wetlands play a complex role in the hydrological cycle. Most of the precipitation which falls on the land is derived from oceanic evaporation and the water eventually returns to the sea through the hydrological cycle; lakes are natural reservoirs in which water is temporarily retained during its passage to the sea.

Depending upon the rate of evaporation and the type of soil, the water in wetlands can percolate downwards towards groundwater aquifers, thus recharging groundwater

Table 1   Distribution and uses of dams in Tanzania

Region	Water Uses			
	Domestic	Livestock	Irrigation	Hydropower
Mwanza	80	-	-	-
Arusha	45	2	-	-
Mara	28	2	1	-
Coast	24	-	-	-
Tabora	20	2	5	-
Shinyanga	18	2	-	-
Singida	18	-	-	-
Mtwara	16	-	-	-
Dodoma	15	-	2	-
Tanga	12	6	1	1
Kilimanjaro	6	6	1	1
Lindi	3	-	-	-
Iringa	3	-	-	1
Morogoro	2	-	-	1
Kagera	1	-	-	-
Mbeya	1	-	-	-
Rukwa	1	-	-	-
Total	293	20	10	4

storage. In areas of high recharge and where surface water sources are contaminated, groundwater is a reliable source of potable water. During the wet season, lakes and floodplains fill with water which is released slowly, thereby helping to reduce flooding downstream.

Although Tanzania is endowed with abundant wetland resources, there has been no systematic national programme for monitoring, development and management of the wetland resources. Most village and urban water supply schemes rely on lakes, small rivers, springs, reservoirs, dams or 'charcos'. The Division of Water Research does not monitor all these small rivers and springs, which are abundant throughout the country, due to financial constraints. However, the Division, on request from the respective Regional Water Engineers, carries out research and investigations on how best the villages can be provided with water. There are over 300 dams and 'charcos' throughout the country (Table 1).

Some of the rivers being monitored have water supply schemes constructed on them, for example, the Ruvu River at the Dar es Salaam-Morogoro Road bridge. However, the majority of the other water sources do not have developed water supply schemes. Nevertheless, continuous monitoring of the stations is necessary to facilitate economic designs for new water supply schemes. Much water resource data is collected from the monitoring network but this information and data become useful only if they are processed and analysed to suit the respective user's needs.

Wetland resources play an important role in the recharge of groundwater storage. Water from these wetlands percolates down to recharge underground storage which can be tapped by the drilling of boreholes. Temporary storage of flood waters, by lakes and floodplains, assists in the reduction and prevention of floods. Sediment carried by rivers is trapped in floodplains.

Conservation of wetlands

It is important that a proper national programme for monitoring and management of these natural water resources is initiated. A water policy should emphasise protection and conservation of all water sources throughout the country, including the preservation of trees around water sources and the promotion of better farming and agricultural methods.

Wetlands can be polluted from various sources, including industrial effluents, domestic sewage and agrochemicals. The application of large quantities of fertiliser, pesticides and herbicides poses a serious threat to downstream water users. Domestic sewage is also a serious source of pollution because very few urban areas treat their domestic effluents. Pollution control is essential in order to prevent contamination of surface water.

High sediment loads, as a result of erosion of the upstream catchment, reduce water quality. Sediments from upstream sources are deposited downstream; these sediments bring fertility to agricultural land but excess quantities have adverse effects, such as loss of useful storage volumes of reservoirs.

It is the Division's intention to initiate a sediment monitoring programme for at least 120 river gauging stations so that the data obtained will be useful in the design of various water development projects. A sediment monitoring programme is essential in the determination of water quality changes. Sediment generated from a watershed can be substantially reduced by applying good land use practices, appropriate disposal of sediment from mining and construction activities, river bank protection, and by instituting a correct programme of reservoir operations.

Conclusions and recommendations

Tanzania is endowed with abundant but uneven water resources. While various types of wetlands are found in Tanzania, only major water bodies are monitored. However, other types of wetlands, such as those found around Lake Manyara, and the Kilombero and Rufiji Valleys, deserve special attention.

Therefore, in order to both conserve and use wetlands as major sources of water supply, the following measures are recommended:

1. All major wetlands must be documented and a monitoring programme initiated to include seasonal variation in the quantity and quality of the water and losses due to evaporation and seepage.

2. Water balance studies of the major wetlands should be undertaken, with a view to facilitating rational utilisation of the water.

3. Existing legislation should cater for the protection and conservation of wetlands as unique ecosystems and sustainable sources of water. This includes ensuring that all existing water sources are protected by the planting of trees, the enforcing of better farming methods around water sources, and by ensuring that untreated effluents are never discharged into wetlands.

Bibliography

Chow, V.T. (Ed.). 1964. *Handbook of Applied Hydrology.* McGraw-Hill, New York.

Mambali, S.S. 1990. Surface water sources - groundwater sources protection and pollution. Paper presented to the Annual Water Engineers Conference, Moshi, 12-17 November, 1990. Ministry of Water, Energy and Minerals.

NEMC/WWF/IUCN. 1990. *Development of a wetland conservation and management programme for Tanzania.* IUCN, Gland, Switzerland. 113 pp.

Irrigation of wetlands in Tanzania

E.H. Masija

Irrigation Department
Ministry of Agriculture, Livestock and Cooperatives
P.O. Box 9192
Dar es Salaam

Summary

Over 1,164,000 ha of wetland areas are listed as suitable for irrigation, mainly for crop production and livestock grazing. Existing and planned irrigation schemes are described for the main river basins where large areas are devoted to rice and sugar cane. Emphasis is placed on the value of small scale, farmer-managed irrigation schemes and the rehabilitation of traditional systems.

Introduction

All wetlands are potentially suitable for agriculture because of their available water and high soil fertility. Due to national priorities or requirements some wetlands are put to other uses, such as game reserves. The total wetland area identified as suitable for irrigation development is estimated to be over 1,164,600 ha (Table 1).

Wetlands are swamps or low lying areas of land which are subject to inundation, usually seasonally. They have hydromorphic soils, transitional morphological characteristics between terrestrial and aquatic ecosystems, and support hydrophytes and halophytes.

Wetlands in Tanzania can be characterised under four main categories:

1. Deltaic processes of rivers which discharge into the Indian Ocean and are characterised by flat topography, low lying relief and heavy clay soils. They are subject to sea water intrusion which contributes to the salinisation of the soils which, under predominantly mangrove vegetation, are potentially acid sulphate.

2. The deltas and lower floodplains of rivers discharging into the major freshwater lakes (Tanganyika, Nyasa and Victoria) are characterised by predominantly heavy, fertile soils, a regular and flat topography, flooding due to high river discharges, and fluctuating lake levels over long periods.

3. The permanent swamps on the periphery of lakes are formed by the outfalls of inland drainage systems, for example Lakes Rukwa, Manyara, Eyasi and the Bahi Swamps. Their topography is regular and flat while their soils are predominantly heavy and affected to some extent by salinity.

4. The floodplains are characterised by fertile, alluvial soils of varying textures, being principally light in the levees and old river channels, and heavy in backswamp areas. Patterns of sedimentation, associated with historic changes in river morphology, result in irregular patterns of deposition; topography is usually regular and mildly sloping.

Table 1   Wetland areas suitable for irrigation

Basin	Total area suitable for irrigation (ha)	% of total area
Rufiji River	628,000	54
Ruvu River	117,000	10
Wami River	169,000	15
Pangani River	25,020	2
Msangasi River	4,800	*
Sigi River	400	*
Umba River	1,040	*
Lake Victoria	98,340	8
Luiche Delta	3,000	*
Manonga River	88,000	8
Ruvuma and Southern Minor Basins	15,000	1
Kyela Plains	15,000	1

* refers to contributions of less than 1%

Utilisation of wetlands

Tanzania's wetlands are chiefly utilised for crop production and livestock in tsetse free areas. The principal livestock keepers are the Sukuma and the Masai. The Sukuma range from the northwest of the country to south of Lake Victoria; they make extensive use of wetlands to the north, south and east of Lake Victoria for dry season grazing. Due to population pressure, they are now starting to move south to the Usangu Plains through the Chunya Corridor. The Masai extend south from the Kenya border to Morogoro Region in Central Tanzania. Their traditional grazing lands were in the north but population pressure has forced them further south and they now utilise the Usangu Plains and Mkata Plains for dry season grazing.

Of the 6 million ha of cultivated land in Tanzania, approximately 450,000 ha is under wetland cultivation. The most important wetland crop is rice, which is grown on 409,000 ha, the remainder is planted with maize, cassava, sweet potatoes, sugar cane and beans. Annual paddy production was 788,300 t in 1988, indicating an average yield of 1.9 t/ha.

For paddy cultivation, flat rice basins are prepared, with or without bunds depending on the water available during the growing season. Farmers living around lakes prepare broad ridges with flat tops in May, when the lake water level drops, and grow sweet potatoes, beans, vegetables or sugar cane. Their counterparts in the Southern Highlands make small earth hills ('vinyungu') on which they plant upland crops.

Cultivation in the wetlands is usually carried out with the hand hoe. Farmers who constantly cultivate wetlands are often poor people without cattle to support the purchase of expensive equipment such as ox ploughs or tractors. Pastoralists usually prefer to utilise their wetlands for cattle grazing. However, in some wetland areas, particularly the Shinyanga and Usangu Plains, pastoralists and tradesmen have embarked on commercial farming. Hence ox ploughs and tractors, which facilitate land preparation, planting and haulage of produce, are increasing. By using such machinery, more land is put under crop production.

Low rainfall, and an outbreak of cassava mealy-bug which destroyed most cassava plants in the Mara Region, has turned attention towards the potential of wetlands for food production. Presently rice, sweet potato and vegetables are grown but low yields are being realised. To increase yields, simple agronomic packages must be developed and the available water must be fully utilised through irrigation.

Irrigation development in wetlands

Traditional irrigation, which is thought to date from the Iron Age, is found on the upland slopes of Mt Kilimanjaro, Mt Meru, the Pare and Usambara Ranges in the north, the Livingstone Ranges in the south, and on the Uluguru Mountains in the east. Irrigation was never practised in the wetlands but traditional flood retention cultivation was carried out in floodplains.

Irrigation development was introduced to wetlands as a result of population pressure on the mountain slopes. Traditional irrigators were forced to settle in low lying areas, where rainfall was less than 400 mm/year, and they used simple technologies to divert water from streams to irrigate their small farms. Eventually, when irrigation became essential to crop production, traditional technologies were improved and expanded.

In the early part of the 20th century, several Baluchi families settled in the Usangu Plains area of Mbeya Region and introduced stream diversion for rice production. This practice was rapidly adopted by the local population and it presently covers some 20,000 ha. Water harvesting and bunding for rice production was introduced in the dry central areas of Tabora, Singida, Shinyanga and Dodoma Regions; the east Biharamulo District in Kagera Region; the south and east of Mwanza; and in the Nyanza Division of Mara Region. This practice, not usually classified as irrigation agriculture, is now estimated to cover 220,000 ha or 53.8% of total area cultivated with rice on the Tanzanian mainland.

In many areas, particularly in the Usangu and Pangani wetlands, the availability of water has become the critical constraint to the expansion of irrigation systems, for which there is considerable demand due to the rapidly increasing local population and high prices for rice. The Irrigation Department is currently undertaking projects aimed at improving agricultural water utilisation in traditional furrow systems and by training farmers in water management and irrigated crop practice. UNDP/FAO are supporting two such projects; one targeted at improving 4,000 ha of irrigated land in Kilimanjaro and Arusha Regions and the other covering 3,000 ha in Usangu Plains. CIDA is supporting a project to improve traditional irrigation systems covering 2,000 ha at Kimani, in the Usangu Plains. Through the Kapunga Project of NAFCO, 1,250 ha of traditional irrigation at Kimara has been improved.

The National Agricultural Policy places emphasis on small scale irrigation schemes and rehabilitation of traditional irrigation systems. These schemes are developed at relatively low cost due to the participation of the beneficiaries in all stages of project development and management, and allows effective training of the farmers on scheme and water management. However, due to the unutilised, vast agricultural potential of the wetlands, the government has taken steps to exploit this potential for large scale irrigation projects. Studies have been conducted in almost all the wetland basins, ranging from identification and feasibility study to full implementation.

Irrigation in the major river basins

Table 2 summarises the area, crop grown and status of irrigation projects in Tanzania. The Rufiji River Basin has 54% of the total potential for wetland agriculture in Tanzania. In 1975, the Government established the Rufiji Basin Development Authority (RUBADA) to plan and direct all development activities in the basin. Several large scale irrigation projects have been studied, completed or are under construction. Water availability is beginning to constrain further

Table 2   Irrigation schemes in Tanzania: status, crops grown and area

Project	Status	Crop	Area (ha)
Rufiji Basin			
Usangu Plains			
Mbarali	operating	rice	3,240
Kapunga	final planning	#	(5,550)
JKT	identified	#	(2,000)
Little Ruaha			
Pawaga	in progress	#	#
Madibra	study complete	rice	(400)
Kilombero Valley			
Kilombero Sugar Co.	operating	sugar	5,240
Chita	operating	rice	500
Mngeta	in progress	rice	5,000 (1,500)
Lower Rufiji			
Ikwiriri Block	in progress	rice	60 (15,000)
Ruvu Basin			
NAFCO	30% operation	#	700
JKT	ceased operation	#	300
Pilot project	surveyed	rice	250
Wami Basin			
Mtibwa	operating	sugar	4,700
Dakawa	operating	rice	2,000
Pangani Basin			
Rehabilitation village schemes	operating	rice	700
Tanga Region			
Kitivo	operating	#	640
Mnazi village	operating	#	150
TRIDEP, 10 schemes	operating	#	40-100 each
Lake Victoria			
Mara River	identified	sugar	(30,000)
Ngono River	identified	rice	(16,000)
Ruvuma Basin			
Maharunga	proposed	#	(8,600)
Chiumo	proposed	#	(1,800)
Nangaramo	proposed	#	(1,100)
Kitele village	proposed	#	(940)
Inland Swamps			
Mto wa mbu, traditional irrigation	operating	#	4,000

Note: figures in brackets are proposed hectarages
       # indicates missing data

development in the Usangu Plains and improved watershed management, irrigation management and environmental conservation is needed. Of the Kilombero Valley Zone, 330,000 ha has been identified as suitable for the irrigated agriculture of rice and sugar cane. In the Lower Rufiji Zone, which includes the river's delta, a pilot irrigation project of 60 ha at Segeni is complete and farmer training for rice production has started.

The total area of the Ruvu River Basin is 85,000 ha and wetlands are found in the 3 km wide floodplain of the Lower Ruvu Valley, between the Ngerengere confluence and the ocean.

Studies by government and FAO identified 51,000 ha in the Wami River Basin as suitable for irrigation. This basin is subject to extensive flooding.

In the Pangani River Basin, wetland areas can mostly be found in the Lower Mkomazi Plains and along various tributaries downstream. Most of the soils are saline but several village level irrigation projects for rice production have been identified.

A total of 6,260 ha has been identified as suitable for irrigation development in various wetlands associated with minor rivers in Tanga. These are in the Msagisi, Sigi and Umba River Basins.

In the Lake Victoria Basin, 61,340 ha of flood land was identified as potentially suitable for irrigation development. The most prominent wetland areas are in the Mara River Basin, in Mara Region, and the vast Ngono River Valley, in Kagera Region. A feasibility study in the Ngono River basin for integrated project development was initiated by the people of Kagera Regions through individual contributions. Two pilot schemes were established at Kyakakera (32 ha) and Nkenge (30 ha) for data collection purposes but neither are now operational due to lack of funds. The entire Ngono River Basin project has been shelved for lack of funds, although the Lutheran Church at Kajunguti has established a centre to cater for small scale farmers being settled in the area. Around the lake, eight small scale irrigation projects (40-120 ha) pump lake water for irrigation in the dry season.

In the Ruvuma River and minor southern basins, a survey of irrigation potential in Mtwara and Lindi Regions was undertaken in 1977 as part of the preparation of an integrated development plan. A total of 15,240 ha was identified as potentially suitable for irrigation development. None of the proposed irrigation projects has been implemented.

Two irrigation schemes are found in the inland lakes and swamps; the Mto wa Mbu flood protection project and the Gichameda Scheme are being developed in the wetlands around Lake Manyara. The latter aims to improve traditional irrigation systems and to control floods in the area.

Simple impoundments

Between 1982 and 1984, with assistance from USAID, the Irrigation Department undertook trials of several impoundment alternatives at the Rift Valley River Project in Dodoma. The most successful of these consisted of roughly levelled

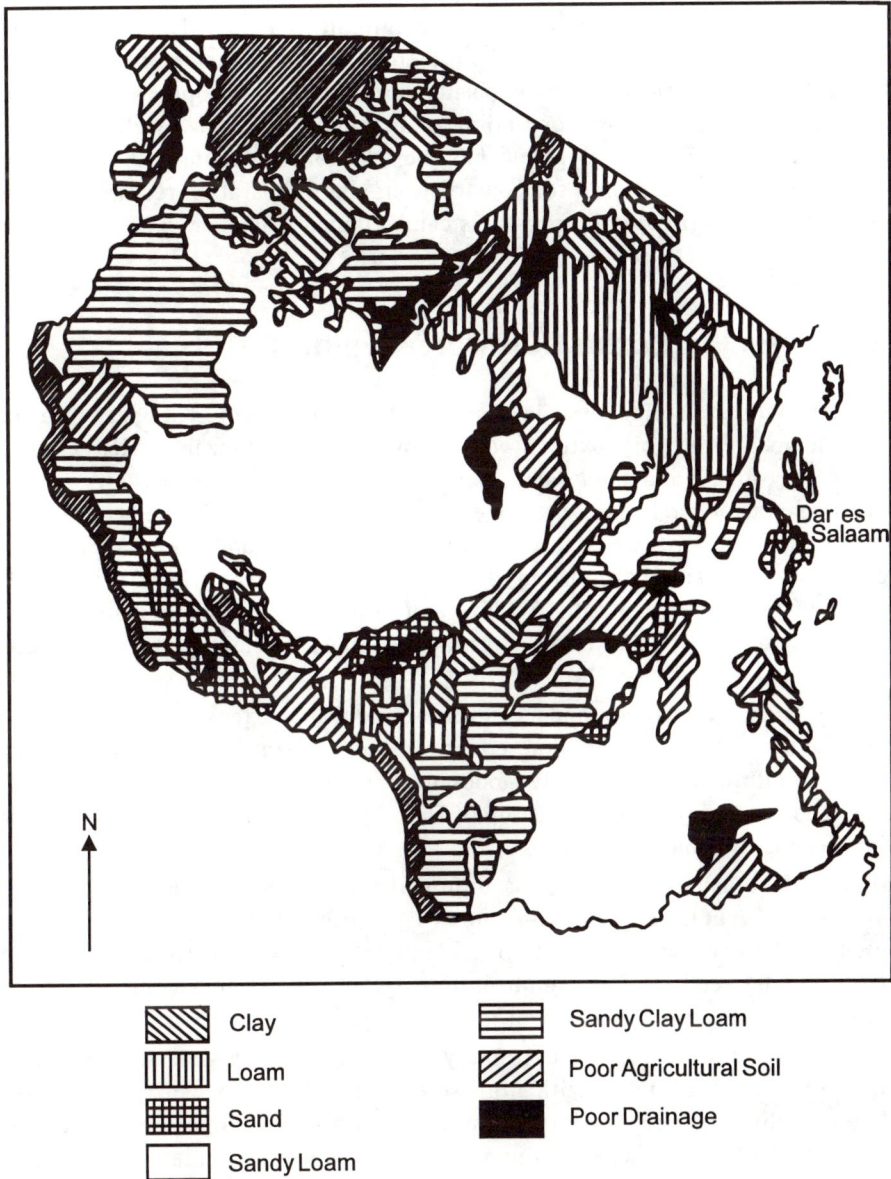

Figure 1   Soil textures of Tanzania

paddies surrounded by substantial bunds constructed by bulldozer, and supplied from stream diversions by simple excavated canals. The pilot area was expanded to 700 ha by 1989 and has consistently produced yields averaging 4 t/ha, even when neighbouring traditional paddies have suffered complete crop failure.

Over the next 6 years, the Irrigation Department plans to expand this form of impoundment to cover 4,000 ha in the low rainfall regions of Dodoma, Singida, Tabora, Shinyanga and Mwanza, where there is already considerable interest on the part of local farmers. Farmer participation in all development stages, and complete farmer control over operations and maintenance, is a key element of the project. This form of development has the additional advantage that, although heavy machinery is required for construction, land preparation requirements are minimal and all agricultural operations can be done by hand.

Soil types, landforms and water regimes

The distribution of soil textures in Tanzania is shown in Figure 1. Loamy-sand and sandy-loam are the soil textures which cover 50% of Tanzania. Heavier soils (clays, clay-loams and sandy-clay loams) make up 30% of the country and are usually characterised by poor drainage and tillage problems. The areas of high soil fertility are largely restricted to soils of volcanic, alluvial and colluvial origin and constitute only a small proportion of the total land area. Elsewhere, the soils are typical of tropical Africa with low levels of nutrients and organic matter. Therefore, fertilisers and sound rotational practices must be employed for good crop yields.

Rolling, hilly and mountainous landforms, requiring extensive intervention to decrease the risks of soil erosion, cover 60% of the country. Undulating, gently sloping landforms, requiring only moderate conservation practices, cover a further 25%. The remaining 15% is made up of flat to gently sloping lands which do not require conservation practices.

Potential land use in Tanzania, based on soil suitability and rainfall is shown in Table 3. The eight land classification units used differentiate between areas of crop potential. A significant feature of this table, in the context of wetlands, is that 19% of the country requires flood control, drainage or special management. Wetland soils are waterlogged seasonally or permanently and are thus poorly aerated.

River flows in Tanzania are extremely variable over the year and high river discharges are associated with high sediment loads. The well defined river channel, which occurs in relatively steep, hilly areas, changes character when it reaches the flatter, low lying topography of the upper floodplain. The velocity of the river decreases, resulting in the deposition of coarse sediment in the river channel and the raising of the river bed. The capacity of the river channel is decreased and the river may break its banks in search of a new course. The upper floodplain is therefore a wide, sand filled area with numerous abandoned old river courses. Further downstream, high flood discharges also cause the

Table 3   Potential land use of Tanzania

Class	Description	Area (thousand ha)	Total area (%)
1	Soils not suitable for cropping	175	0.2
2	Soils where little cropping is possible	7,850	8.9
3	Fertile soils where low rainfall or shallow rooting depth limits crop yield	4,070	4.6
4	Soils of very low fertility with moderate potential	29,665	33.6
5	Soils of medium fertility with moderate potential	20,010	22.7
6	Soils of medium to high fertility with high potential	8,075	9.1
7	Soils of low fertility in areas of high rainfall	2,515	2.8
8	Alluvial or colluvial soils of considerable potential but often requiring flood control, drainage or special management	15,980	18.9
	Total land area	88,340	100.0

Note: 22% of land has adequate rainfall for crop production; that is over 750 mm in 9 years out of 10

river to overtop its banks and coarse materials are deposited in the immediate vicinity of the river channel. The gradual reduction of water velocity, as it enters the lower floodplain, results in a similar reduction in the size of materials deposited. As a result, the floodplain in its middle and lower sections reflects a characteristic landscape pattern: a narrow river levee composed of coarser textured materials lying above the general floodplain level; a medium textured and moderately well to imperfectly drained transition zone; and a lower basin of clay soils with poor drainage and swampy areas.

Usually the effect of a water regime on soil characteristics is dependent on the soil drainage. At the river outfalls of the inland drainage systems (Lakes Rukwa, Eyasi, Manyara, and the Bahi Swamp), the soils are influenced by highly saline ground-water. Further upstream, soil salinity decreases as it is affected by wet season leaching and a lower dry season water table. A similar phenomenon occurs in the deltas of rivers discharging into the Indian Ocean. Salinity of wetlands occurring on the upper reaches of rivers is invariably associated with impeded drainage. This is particularly so in the upper reaches of the Pangani River where a layer of hard pan, thought to be associated with an old lake bed, occurs at shallow depth.

Intervention, maintenance and management of wetlands

Wetlands require human intervention in order to sustain high crop yields over an extended period. Invariably, wetland cultivation in the country is characterised by the lack of an organised farmer programme. Every farmer will have his own cropping calendar and choice of crops grown, and water use is inadequately controlled.

In some areas of traditional irrigation, customary laws are used and all the activities and maintenance is under farmer's control. An irrigation committee is selected and sub- committees formed for the various aspects of the traditional system. The organisation of routine maintenance and water allocation is the responsibility of the committees and sub-committees. Assistance for major repairs to these systems is usually channelled to the villages by regional authorities from their respective development funds.

The Lower Moshi (Rau River) Project is an example of an institutionally managed smallholder scheme. Farmers are organised in water users groups, each with 30 ha. These groups are responsible for operation and maintenance at tertiary block level but the main and secondary systems are the responsibility of the project extension unit of the government. The development cost of this project was US$ 15,000/ha and there has been no attempt at loan recovery. The scheme is heavily subsidised by the government; while tractor hire rates are at commercial levels, operation and maintenance charges only cover a small proportion of actual costs.

The present philosophy concerning cost recovery of such schemes is that farmers should contribute labour and locally available materials (sand, rocks) whereas the government should provide (free of charge) expertise, machinery and other mate-rials. Operation and maintenance should be the responsibility of farmers while the government should assist with the formation and training of farmer organisations to undertake these duties. These organisations should levy charges on their mem-bers to finance major maintenance requirements.

Constraints affecting irrigation development in wetlands

The lack of financial assistance to purchase heavy earth moving equipment and agricultural machinery hampers the development of irrigation projects.

Technical constraints involve the following:

- lack of experienced personnel to carry out feasibility studies and engineering designs of projects and to organise formation of farmers' organisations;
- inadequate data for planning, designing and operation of irrigation projects in wetlands;
- lack of adequate agronomic packages applicable to wetlands.

Social constraints involve the following:

- traditional cultivation customs in some parts restrict people from cultivating wet soils and from growing new crops;
- in some areas of Tanzania, customs and culture regard wetland cultivation as being the role of women, whose available time is committed to other duties. This hinders expansion of wetland agricultural development.

Recommendations for irrigation development in wetlands

To attain the agricultural potential of wetlands, sufficient funds for their development should be made available by the government.

A National Technical Cooperation Network for Wetland Development (NWEDEM) should be established. Among other duties, NWEDEM will coordinate data collection of wetlands and provide a forum for solving the above constraints. FAO should assist the individual countries in setting up National Units of NWEDEM.

Bibliography

Agrar- und Hydrotechnik (AHT). 1982. Irrigated agricultual development in the lower Rufiji Valley. Feasibility study. Report prepared by AHT (West Germany).

Instrupa, Hydroplan and Redec. 1982. Lower Mkomazi irrigation project feasibility study. Report prepared by Instrupa, Hydroplan and Redec Consultant Engineers.

United Republic of Tanzania (URT). 1967. *Atlas of Tanzania.* URT, Dar es Salaam.

United Republic of Tanzania (URT). 1982. The National Agricultural Policy. Final report. Ministry of Agriculture.

Pollution of wetlands in Tanzania

S. Mkuula

National Environment Management Council
P.O. Box 63154
Dar es Salaam

Summary

Pollution of wetlands is becoming a serious concern, due mainly to the rapid increase of human development activities. Although most extensive wetlands are in remote places where the human activities which lead to pollution of the environment are minimal, some have become polluted by waste products related to development activities or human survival.

In this paper, major types of pollution from human activities are considered, including urbanisation, industrialisation, mining, agricultural activities and oil pollution.

Proposals for combating pollution problems in wetlands are discussed with a focus on policy, planning and legislation; administration and institutional support; environmental research and technology; and improving information, environmental education and public awareness.

Finally, the paper highlights some approaches and techniques for pollution prevention.

Introduction

Pollution can be defined as any action or condition impinging on land, air or water, which is detrimental to health, sanitation or the public interest. In Tanzania, the major types of pollution related to human activity can be classified as caused by urbanisation, industrialisation, mining activities, the use of chemicals and oil spills.

In this paper, the term wetland covers estuaries, coasts, lakes, swamp forests, floodplains, freshwater marshes and peatlands.

The extent of the pollution problem

The majority of wetlands in Tanzania are not polluted. The main reason for this is that the most extensive wetlands are in remote places where the human activities which lead to pollution are minimal. In other localities, activities undertaken in the quest for development or survival have caused pollution.

Wetlands which have become victims of pollution are mostly adjacent to the following localities:

- urban centres;
- areas close to large polluting industries, such as sisal processing;
- areas where mining is a major means of income generation;
- areas where pesticide application is extensive.

Pollution resulting from urbanisation

Although Tanzania is one of the least urbanised countries in the world, the rate of growth of its urban population is one of the highest. The extremely low standard of sanitation and sewage in all of Tanzania's urban centres is cause for concern. The fast urbanisation process taking place in the country has far reaching and mostly negative impacts, affecting all urban dwellers. Air, water, solid wastes and oil pollution are rapidly increasing and have dramatic consequences on the life and health of the urban users of the wetlands.

As in other countries, the majority of large urban centres in Tanzania occur in or near wetlands; Dar es Salaam, Tanga, Mwanza, Zanzibar, Morogoro and Arusha are all associated with wetlands.

Water pollution due to liquid waste

Water pollution has become a common problem and a cause for concern in all urban areas in Tanzania, particularly during the rainy seasons. Every year outbreaks of water-related diseases, such as cholera and diarrhoea, are reported. Most serious is the contamination of drinking water sources with pollutants and bacteria.

One of the main sources of water pollution in urban wetlands is domestic and institutional wastes. Only eight towns on the Tanzanian mainland have access to sewage systems. When septic tanks and soak-aways are included, only 15-20% of the population has an efficient means of human waste disposal. A study of urban waste disposal was carried out in Dar es Salaam by Haskoning and M-Konsult in 1988 who found that only 6% of the total population of 1,723,000 was served by the city sewage system. Around 80% of the unsewered proportion depended on on-site sanitary facilities such as pit latrines or septic tanks. The remaining 20% lacked elementary sanitary facilities and the majority of these had no water supply. Currently, untreated sewage from the city centre is discharged into the sea close to the coast; in some areas, sewage undergoes some inadequate treatment while the rest of the town has either no treatment plants at all or facilities which are not functioning. Drainage systems for surface run off is found in limited areas only.

Due to the generally poor sanitary standard, most of the local receiving water bodies, including adjacent soils and coastal waters, are heavily polluted. Where investigations have been carried out, such as the Msimbazi River in Dar es Salaam, the presence of substantial amounts of organic matter, nutrients and chemical pollutants has been reported. Bacteriological investigations show that human faecal contamination of river water makes it unsuitable for domestic use, swimming or for irrigation of vegetables. Waste from urban animal industry has significantly contributed to pollution of the soils and water bodies, particularly with nitrates.

Pollution due to solid wastes

Solid wastes constitute one of the most obvious pollution problems in Tanzanian urban centres. Systems for collecting domestic, institutional and industrial solid wastes exist in all the towns but these systems are operating at very low efficiencies. The result is the unregulated piling up of the waste. Dar es Salaam provides a good example of low waste collection efficiency; about 64% of the waste in the city centre is collected. For the major part of the city only 13% of the waste is removed; in areas which are not served at all, wastes are usually buried or burned.

Methods of disposal of the wastes do not meet the required minimum standards and wastes are often crudely dumped together, irrespective of their nature or state. The solid wastes accumulating at such dump sites are a source of pollution of the soil, and surface and groundwaters.

Air pollution

As the urban centres grow, so does the construction industry which involves excavation and transportation of stones, sand, cement and other building materials. These activities, together with the actual processing of the materials at building sites, increase the levels of airborne dust and predispose people to respiratory complaints.

Motor vehicles and other forms of transportation are notorious for polluting the air in towns and cities. This can clearly be witnessed in Dar es Salaam which has narrow roads, few open spaces and a congestion of heavily polluting vehicles. Cars and motorcycles produce large quantities of nitrogen oxides and carbon monoxide, the later being very poisonous, especially to infants, pregnant women and the elderly. The gasoline processed and used in Tanzania has a high concentration of lead, one of the most toxic elements.

The burning of solid waste has contributed to the worsening state of air pollution in the urban areas.

Pollution resulting from industrial processes

Industries are major sources of water, air and soil pollution. About 80% of all of Tanzania's industries are located in urban areas. Distinguishable from domestic, institutional and other sources of pollution, industrial wastes may contain heavy metals like mercury, chromium, lead and cadmium; salts of cyanide, nitrite and nitrate; organic matter, micro-organisms and nutrients; and toxic chemicals such as pesticides. By international standards, Tanzanian industries are highly polluting, the main reasons being that there are very few industries in the country which have incorporated provisions for treating the wastes they generate and the factories have been built without including technologies which help to reduce waste.

It is encouraging to note that the general public is becoming increasingly aware and sensitive to pollution of their surroundings, particularly when toxic pollutants are involved. The recent public uproar over the Tabata dump and the now-under-construction Moshi Pesticides Project are reminders that more care needs to be taken in selecting sites and pollution management.

Water pollution

Water pollution is the most widespread pollution problem in Tanzania. Pollution of water bodies with industrial effluents occurs in rivers, lakes and estuaries in the industrialised areas. The industries which discharge effluents of serious and immediate environmental concern are those involved in tanning, petrochemicals, sisal, pesticides formulation, asbestos, metal processing, battery manufacture, textiles, foam production, and paint and plastic manufacture.

Some of the more important valleys, lakes and rivers which are polluted with industrial waste are the Msimbazi River in Dar es Salaam, Ngerengere River in Morogoro, Themi River in Arusha, Lake Victoria at Mwanza, Bukoba and Musoma, Rivers Karanga, Njoro and Rau near Moshi, and River Kiwira in Tukuyu District.

Air pollution

The most important industrial air pollutants include sulphur dioxide, nitrogen oxides and hydrocarbons. The oil refinery and the cement plant in Dar es Salaam, the cement and fertiliser plants in Tanga, and the Kiwira coal power station in Tukuyu District are well known cases of industrial air pollution situated in wetlands and are among the main producers of sulphur dioxide. The people living close to these industries are becoming aware of the environmental and health hazards they are likely to suffer. In some areas of Tanga municipality, the high incidence of respiratory disease is possibly due to emissions from the fertiliser factory.

Pollution arising from industrial solid wastes

Collection, and especially disposal, of industrial solid wastes is of a poor standard in Tanzania. Hazardous industrial waste is usually mixed with ordinary industrial and urban solid wastes and disposed of crudely at selected or illegal dump sites. In the Tabata solid wastes dump in Dar es Salaam, both hazardous and ordinary waste is dumped, causing a national outcry. A recent survey of some of the major industries in the country has shown an alarming situation. At a large tannery, there are heaps of chromium tanned leather dumped outside the factory walls. Surface runoff transports toxic chemicals from these heaps into the nearby river which is used by people and animals.

Pollution resulting from mining activities

Pollution arising from mining and mining based activities is quite marked and is rapidly increasing in various parts of Tanzania. With liberalisation of trade, Tanzania has witnessed a drastic increase in small scale mining activities over the past few years. Pollution is becoming an increasingly serious problem in the major mining areas. Such areas include the gold mining zone around Lake Victoria; Mpanda; Chunya; coal mining in Kiwira, Tukuyu District; tin mining in Korogwe; ruby mining near Morogoro; tanzanite and phosphate mines in Arusha Region; limestone mines in Dar es Salaam, Tanga and Mbeya Regions; and salt mining along the coastal belt. With the advent of drilling for natural gas and possibly oil in the coastal zone, there may be profound negative impacts on the especially fragile marine and coastal wetlands. In the organised, large scale mining sector, environmental impact should be relatively easy to prevent and control. However, unorganised and uncontrolled small scale mining is doing tremendous damage to the environment.

Overburden is the main solid waste generated by the mining industry. The fraction of useful commodity is usually very small, and the remainder is rock and soil waste which is dumped without concern for the environment.

Pollution of water

Solids and colloidal materials from overburden are often responsible for increased sedimentation in the adjacent water bodies. Due to erosion of tailings dumps, the ground and surface water is contaminated with toxic substances. At low pH values, heavy metals (iron, manganese, cadmium, zinc, aluminium) can create serious water pollution problems. In Tanzania, most gold is extracted from the soil using mercury, a toxic substance which contaminates soil and water. Between April 1990 and July 1991, private miners sold 3.53 t of gold to the Bank of Tanzania (*Uhuru*, 2 Sept. 1991) and it is estimated that 4 t of mercury was used to extract this gold.

Pollution of the air

Much of the air pollution observed in the mining centres is due to soil and rock dust produced during mining, haulage, crushing and grinding of ore material. Dust clouds are produced by wind from tailings dumps. In small scale mining, grinding of the ore is done with wooden mortars and workers are exposed to high concentrations of silica dust which causes respiratory disease.

Pollution resulting from use of pesticides

Tanzania uses a lot of pesticides in public health programmes and in agriculture to control diseases and to improve farm yields. Most of the pesticides used in the country are imported.

Pesticides pose environmental pollution problems when they are discharged into the environment because they are poisonous to many non-target species. Some pesticides remain active for long periods or may break down into more toxic compounds. Excessive importation of pesticides into Tanzania causes a surplus which becomes expired and is then dumped or stored. Surveys have shown that there are large stocks of expired pesticides in the country, especially in the coffee and cotton growing areas. These, together with the residues of pesticides already applied to fields and buildings, pose a danger to human health and the environment. Other sources of pesticide pollution stem from poor storage and transportation and inadequate management of manufacturing and formulating plants. Lack of awareness of the dangers linked to the handling of pesticides further complicates the problem.

Water is the main receiver of pesticide pollutants. Approximately 50% of the pesticide sprayed onto a crop falls on the ground or is carried away by wind and enters the water table *via* rain or irrigation waters. Some pesticides eventually contaminate drinking water. Expired pesticides also find their way into the soil and water bodies.

Oil pollution

Pollution of water bodies and soil with oil is becoming a major problem, especially in the urban areas. Wherever oil is used and handled, such as in garages and workshops, the ground at the site and nearby ponds, trenches or ditches are impregnated with oil through discharge of oily wastes or accidental spills. Car washing businesses are often sited near streams or ponds, leaving waters covered with layers of oil. At the ports, large quantities of oil are handled and there is a chance of large scale oil spills from ships. One major oil spill occurred at Dar es Salaam harbour in 1984.

It is economically feasible to collect and reprocess waste oil, thus saving the country foreign exchange and minimising pollution. Unfortunately, these practical measures to control waste oil are non-existent in Tanzania.

Industries and diesel powered electricity generators in Tanzania are renowned for discharges of waste oil into the environment. Recently, Lake Victoria was polluted by waste oil from electricity generators in Bukoba and Mwanza.

Proposals for improving the pollution problem in wetlands

Policy, planning and legislation

It is important that the government gives priority to policies which involve environmental protection. Environmental considerations must be incorporated into the planning of all major projects as a fundamental requirement. All major development projects should be preceded by environmental impact assessments as preventive action is the cheapest and most effective pollution control. Pollution-related, sectoral legislation needs to be revised with a view to harmonising and updating it to take into account the current situation. Comprehensive and more powerful environmental laws should be formulated and enacted. Enabling the relevant bodies to enforce such legislation, by supplying them with the appropiate resources, as legislation which is not enforced is worse than no legislation at all.

Administrative and institutional support

The main problem relating to administrative and institutional arrangements is the lack of coordination and cooperation between sectors or bodies concerned with pollution control. The government should facilitate the work of such sectors through budgetary allocations, manpower and facilities. In some cases, such as solid waste management, the division of responsibilities is not clearly defined, therefore, a department should be formed to specifically deal with these areas. There is also a need to strengthen cooperation among directly concerned institutions, in order to promote effective coordination of industrial pollution control issues. Existing industrial pollution problems can be dealt with only through concerted efforts and actions.

Environmental research and technology

The government should encourage environmental research and technological innovation as a priority in its attempt to alleviate environmental pollution. Research on clean and waste reducing technologies should be given due consideration. Institutions engaged in environmental management and technological innovations, as well as industries and other entities showing sympathy to environmental issues, should be supported in order to encourage approaches aimed at preventing pollution.

Improving information, environmental education and public awareness

It is imperative to understand the causes and effects of pollution problems and to devise ways and means for their solution and prevention, based on viewing humanity as an integral part of the environment. Thus environmental education has to play a vital role in building public awareness. Environmental education, both formal and informal, will inculcate the habits of preservation and conservation of nature in the general public. It is extremely important to equip people with the necessary knowledge, skills, attitude and motivation for the prevention of pollution and resource deterioration. There is also an urgent need for research and technology advancement institutions, and environmental management bodies, to establish pollution monitoring programmes. Information generated will in turn facilitate assessment of the environmental impacts of different activities. Results of assessments will further be used as a base for deciding which appropriate technology will be adopted for pollution abatement.

Methods of pollution control

Urban pollution

There is a need to adopt a community-based approach to controlling urban pollution, in view of the limited financial resources available. Many of the current problems, especially drainage and refuse handling, can be solved if people actually participate in keeping their surroundings clean.

Machinery and equipment which are economical with water should be encouraged. The potential for recycling of liquid and solid waste should be assessed.

Industrial pollution

There is an obvious need to rehabilitate the existing, dilapidated industries and plants. The existing technologies need to be updated to minimise wastes, product losses, water consumption and energy use. Recycling of wastes and adoption of cleaner or low waste technologies should be emphasised. Rehabilitation packages should include methods for treating final wastes and the training of plant operators in the reduction of waste.

Mining pollution

There is need for the government to organise small scale miners into cooperatives which should be supported with administrative and technical expertise to better control their activities and minimise environmental pollution. Mining activities in new sites should be preceded by an environmental impact assessment.

There is need to introduce and promote recycling techniques in small scale gold mining centres so that mercury pollution is minimised. The Tan Can Gold Company of Igunga, Tabora has already set an example by recycling mercury. Panning or washing ore minerals in or near water sources should be avoided.

Public awareness campaigns, especially in the mining centres, should be launched so that people can learn the health problems associated with such activities and how to protect themselves from them.

Pesticide pollution

First and foremost, the government should ensure that purchasing, distribution and selling procedures which lead to accumulation of unused pesticide stocks are minimised. Expired pesticides and containers should be disposed of in an environmentally safe manner. Handling of pesticides, by the manufacturer, the handler and the applicator, should be carried out correctly. To facilitate this educational programmes are needed.

Pesticides should be stored in properly designed and maintained areas which are manned by staff trained in pesticide handling. Pesticide containers should be correctly and adequately labelled and the provision of instructions for their safe handling should be mandatory.

Bibliography

Ak'habuhaya, J.L.and M. Lodenius. Pesticides in Tanzania. Department of Environmental Conservation. University of Helsinki. Publ. No. 10. 135 pp.

Mkuula, S.S. and F.M.T. Mpendazoe. Disposal of Industrial wastes in Tanzania. *Proceeding of the first workshop in preparation of a National Conservation Strategy for Tanzania.* 12-17 November, Dodoma. NEMC, SIDA. pp.126-146.

Mutalemwa, A.M. Handling of sewerage and refuse in urban areas in Tanzania. *Proceeding of the first workshop in preparation of a National Conservation Strategy for Tanzania.* 12-17 November, Dodoma. NEMC, SIDA. pp.147-163.

Nanyaro, J.T. Environmental impacts of mining, quarrying and oil exploitation with special reference to Tanzania. *Proceeding of the first workshop in preparation of a National Conservation Strategy for Tanzania. 12-17 November, Dodoma.* NEMC, SIDA. pp. 164-184.

Social and cultural values of wetlands in Tanzania

C.K. Omari

Sociology Department
University of Dar es Salaam
P.O. Box 35029
Dar es Salaam

Summary

The socio-economic aspects of wetland farming and fisheries are discussed together with the cultural values of wetlands such as scenery, sources of traditional medicine, and diseases. The socio-political features of wetland life are mentioned as well as the international considerations of wetland water needs. A plea is made for more research into indigenous knowledge of wetland values and products.

Introduction

Wetlands are important natural resources which provide water to living creatures. People living near wetlands have developed socio-cultural values around the wetlands which are part of the people's history and current existence.

This paper takes a social-developmental approach to wetlands. It describes and analyses some of the socio-cultural value systems that have developed and become part of the lives of societies living around wetlands. It briefly examines the future of these natural resources, given the destructive culture which has developed globally.

Background information

In geographical and geological terms, wetlands are freshwater swamps, coastal swamps, mangroves, floodplains and lake edges. They also include water sources like springs and basins which are always the centre of those political and social organisations which form the value system of the people associated with these resources.

There are 51,000 km^2 of inland waters in Tanzania, including the large lakes such as Victoria, Tanganyika, Nyasa and Rukwa, and rivers such as Rufiji, Ruvu, Pangani, Kagera, Malagarasi and Wami (United Republic of Tanzania, 1967). There are over 10,000 ponds and reservoirs on the mainland. The coastal area of Tanzania extends 1,300 km along the Indian Ocean (NEMC/WWF/IUCN, 1990).

There are extensive river basins in Tanzania. For example, the Malagarasi basin covers about 126,000 km^2, the Wembere and Eyasi basins cover 65,500 km^2; the Rufiji basin covers 177,500 km^2; the Wami River basin covers about 20,100 km^2; the Pangani River basin covers 29,500 km^2 and the Ruvu River basin covers 18,400 km^2. At the same time many areas of Tanzania experience long periods of dry weather and much of the arid regions are sparsely populated. The uneven water distribution in Tanzania was recognised from the time of the German administration and there was a plan to draw water from Lake Victoria to alleviate shortages in Central Tanzania.

The use and misuse of wetlands is related to the availability of water among the people. Discussing use of water in Africa, Jarret (1979) concluded that there was a need for adequate water control since about 30% of the continent received less than 250 mm annually.

The values of wetlands to people

The following sections discuss the value systems that people tend to develop as they try to manage and control their environment and resources, in this case wetlands.

The socio-economic values of wetlands

Wetlands have been, and are, the basis of community economic activities. People who live within or around wetlands have, for a long time, been involved in various economic activities and their settlement patterns have been influenced by the wetlands.

Farming

Farming activities are the major economic pursuits around wetlands with the cultivation of crops such as paddy, maize and various types of vegetables and fruits. The practice of growing rice in swamps is increasing in many countries of Africa, led by Egypt; between 1974 and 1975, Tanzania produced 160,000 t of paddy (Jarret, 1979).

The farming activities in floodplains are controlled by the seasonal floods. People who live and farm in some floodplains move to higher lands during the floods and return to the valleys during the cultivation season. In fact some people, like those in the lower Rufiji floodplain, have developed a 'two homes' system. They live in one house during the cultivation season and the other during the flood season. This type of settlement pattern has traditionally enabled the peasants to cultivate two types of crops. Some crops are planted when the areas are still wet but the water level is falling (flood recession agriculture). The use of such seasonal floodplains allows the planting of a range of crops; paddy is planted in standing water as the water level falls, while quick growing crops (such as cucumber and tomato) are planted later in damp soil. In this way, wetlands of this type influence not only settlement patterns but economic activities as well. The people adapt themselves to the seasons and organise their various activities accordingly. The disadvantage of this type of settlement pattern is that people cannot build permanent houses but must move their habitation between the flood-plain and the uplands. It was on this basis that in the 1970s, at the peak of the implementation of 'Ujamaa' programmes, the people in the Rufiji floodplain were moved by force to the uplands for their own safety.

The ownership of land in these areas follows the traditional land tenure system. The family land, where family members have been living and cultivating for a long time, is passed to the next generation. If members of the family want to cultivate new areas, they normally follow the community based land tenure system whereby the land which does not belong to a specific family or clan can be assigned to those in need.

Traditionally, only subsistence farming took place in wetlands but with the intro-duction of the money economy peasants have also been producing for market. For example, peasant production contributes a significant percentage towards Tanza-nia's paddy production and these smallholders help the country to meet its food production targets. In swampy areas, peasants normally cultivate at the edges of the water, using various crops such as paddy and maize. Such cultivation is found in the Malagarasi and Kagera Basins.

Fishing

Another important economic activity in wetlands is fishing. Jackson (1975) esti-mated that 51,000 km^2 of freshwater and 10,000 family fishponds produce 83% of Tanzania's total fish catch by weight and 60% by value (40% of the total value was from Lake Victoria alone). Tilapia was the major fish (35%) caught in Lake Victoria (Jackson, 1975) but it is likely that this percentage has been reduced due to the introduction of nile perch.

In Lake Tanganyika, the fishing of *dagaa*, a fresh water sardine (*Stolothlorissa tanganyikae*), has been carried out for both local consumption and export, mostly to Zambia (Jackson, 1975). Demand for fish meal, made from *dagaa* for use in the stockfeed industry, may affect the economics of the fishery by increasing the price of *dagaa* beyond the scope of the poor.

People's nutritional status is often threatened by commercialisation of the fishing industry as fishermen often sell the whole catch, retaining none for home consump-tion, or prices rise so the poor can no longer afford to eat fish.

In the past, fishing by peasants was carried out using traditional technology. Most of the methods used were not harmful to non-target species but the recent use of dynamite, especially in the coastal areas, threatens the aquatic environment and thus a major part of the people's diet.

The commercialisation of the prawn fishery has made the coastal areas of Tanzania, especially the Rufiji Delta, places where foreign trawlers are found. Some of these trawlers fish indiscriminately, being interested only in total catch, and they may deplete the prawn fishery which is a natural resource and part of Tanzania's wealth.

Medicinal, scientific and aesthetic values of wetlands

Some wetland trees, grass, leaves and flowers have been used as traditional medicines by the local people. The value of medicinal trees associated with wetlands is being studied by collaboration between researchers and traditional doctors, 'waganga', at Muhimbili College of Health Sciences, Traditional Medicine Centre.

At the University of Dar es Salaam, the Department of Botany is carrying out research on marine algae, which show promise as an export crop and for use in local industry.

Wetlands are green throughout the year and attract various birds and animals. They have their own unique and balanced environments. Such areas are attractive to both local and foreign visitors and have become tourist centres. The coastal areas provide places where people go to enjoy swimming, picnics and parties. When these environments are developed and conserved, they become a source of income and recreation and are a pride to the nation.

Everyone in Tanzania has the right to recreational facilities. Young and old, men and women need places to exercise this aspect of their rights. Wetlands provide that opportunity. However, wetlands may harbour hazards to the communities in their vicinity; besides the danger of floods, water-associated insects, such as mosquitoes, can spread malaria and elephantiasis, and snails spread bilharzia.

The socio-cultural aspects of wetlands

Political and cultural organisation

The political organisation of the people living near or around wetlands is governed by the existing social structures. The socio-economic activities carried out by the people in such areas do, to some extent, influence their socio-political life. The main economic activities of the people living near or around wetlands are fishing and farming. In both economic systems, the political life of the people, especially at community level, may be looked at as the management of resources and the decision making processes.

In general, the societies living around or near wetlands are not separated totally from the life of many of the ethnic groups living in the uplands. For example, people living on the Rufiji River and coastal areas are patrilineal in their family social structures and their socio-political structures may be similar to nearby communities. Thus, the management of resources, be it fishing or land availability, is controlled by men, and women have little influence on those resources. As Swantz (1985) has shown in her research on women's position in Tanzanian society, women do not own the means of production or productive forces although they use them when developing the family's properties and wealth. The customary inheritance system determines the ownership and control of land.

Most of the women in wetlands participate in economic activities according to the assigned roles and divisions of labour which are normally based on gender. In a fishing village, men go into the deep waters to fish while women participate in fishing activities in the shallows but once the fish have been brought ashore, both men and women participate in selling them. As in other economic activities, men tend to dominate in the matter of dispersal of income obtained from the sale of fish. There are very few fisherwomen in Tanzania. Around Nyumba ya Mungu Dam in Kilimanjaro Region, many women are involved in the fishing business. These women may own the fishing gear and transport facilities, and travel to Dar es Salaam to sell their fish but, in many cases, women cannot participate in the actual fishing. It is, therefore, very important that research on women's involvement in fishing activities around or near wetlands be carried out.

In order to have control of the resources found in wetlands, local development in the management and control of resources must be emphasised. The collapse of TAFICO (Tanzania Fishing Company) was a warning that the fishing industry must be supported through the development of human resources, technology and marketing venues. Without such development, the control of the fishery resource in wetlands will remain in the hands of the powerful minority while the local people, who are the majority, and owners - women included - become toiling workers only.

Management of national resources

To understand the international politics related to wetlands, there is a need to look into the existing commercial and business licences. Tanzania's natural resources associated with wetlands should be utilised for the development of the indigenous people rather than foreign companies. In the wake of trade liberalisation, anything produced in Tanzania should reduce its foreign debt and develop its economy. Natural resource exploitation must be planned so that Tanzania gets its rightful share in world business and economic development.

There must be development of appropriate technology to develop and exploit the natural resources available in Tanzania's wetlands. For example, marine algae has potential use in local industry as well as its foreign market value but such a product needs to be developed for the local industry with appropriate technology. Without this the possibility of being exploited is very high and the people of Tanzania may lose the power to control and manage their own natural resource.

Finally, the sensitive issue of the use of water from Lake Victoria to irrigate dry parts of central Tanzania should be discussed. Germany had a long term vision of making Tabora the central administrative centre for their Eastern Africa Colonial Empire, which included Rwanda, Burundi and part of Zaire. After independence, the plan to draw water from Lake Victoria was not implemented, due to geo-political reasons; any reduction of water flow to Lake Victoria, and thus the River Nile, would affect Uganda's electricity production and agricultural systems in Sudan and Egypt. The effect of water extraction needs to be re-examined as Lake Victoria gets its water from many sources and harnessing some of this water for the development of the people in Tanzania could be one way for the Tanzanian people to control and manage their own natural resources. The cost of such a project would be high, but worthwhile attempting if political development and empowerment of the people to control their own natural resources is to become meaningful. The geo-politics involved in such a development could be solved without ruining any country's economic development.

The future of wetlands

The future of wetlands depends on how much people change their attitudes towards environment preservation and management. Human survival and wellbeing depend on the successful development of sustainable global ethics; economic growth and environment protection should go hand in hand (World Commission of Environment and Development, in Engel, 1990, p.1).

Natural resources belong to the whole community; they were used in the past development of communities and will do so in the future (Omari, 1990) but sometimes development projects and programmes using non-Tanzanian experts do not take this into consideration. Very often the local people are overlooked or blamed for causing desertification through poor cultivation and inappropriate animal husbandry methods. Very infrequently are criticisms leveled against the experts who participate in the environmental destruction in the name of development. The pollution of our wetlands is not brought about by peasants but by the developers. For example, industries are established without appropriate systems for the disposal of waste products which flow into rivers, oceans and lakes, destroying wetland environments. The wetland areas of the Msimbazi River in Dar es Salaam and the sources of water in lower Moshi, lower Arusha and Tanga are polluted, because of developments upstream.

The harvesting of timber to earn foreign exchange is affecting some water sources. Foreign experts have recommended the introduction of exotic species of trees to our catchment forests with adverse environmental effects. In the Arumeru Forests project, the need for foreign exchange caused exotic trees from cold climates to be planted, on the advice of foreign experts. The trees grew quickly but certain questions were not addressed. The long term effects of the project, especially in relation to sources of water which once fed the wetlands near Mount Meru, have not been analysed. There are socio-economic problems which need to be investigated and their results made public. If they are not made public we are violating the rights of the people who used to profit from those wetlands.

Conclusion

This paper has sought to describe and analyse the values of the people associated with wetlands in Tanzania. I conclude that wetlands have existed for a long time and have been utilised by the local people for their sustenance. Wetlands are a resource of the Tanzanian people and they should be used for the benefit of the nation.

The paper has shown briefly that there are environmental problems related to the current development of wetlands and we should guard against the destruction of these wetlands.

In conclusion, the following question should be asked. How can we cooperate to educate decision makers that the destruction of wetlands is the destruction of the social lives of the people who live near or around these areas? Many living creatures make up the ecosystem and if it is disturbed it will also affect us socially, economically, politically and culturally. It must, therefore, be the task of everyone to develop and preserve the wetlands rather than destroy them in any way that may advance certain people or social groups.

Finally, there is a need to study and evaluate the indigenous knowledge of wetlands. People living around or near the wetlands have had an opportunity to develop knowledge about fauna, trees and rocks through their experience. Such knowledge should be retained for future use in the community.

Bibliography

Berry, L. 1975. Utilization of Water Resources. Pages 74-75. In: L. Berry (Ed.). *Tanzania in Maps*. University of London Press, London.

Engel, J.R. 1990. Introduction: The ethics of sustainable development. Pages 1-23. In: J.R. Engel and J.G. Engel (Eds). *Ethics of Environment and Development: Global Challenge and International Response*. Belhaven Press, London.

Jackson, I.J. 1975. Fisheries. Pages 66-67. In: L. Berry (Ed.). *Tanzania in Maps*. University of London Press, London.

Jarret, H.R. 1979. *Africa*. MacDonald and Evans Ltd, Plymouth.

NEMC/WWF/IUCN. 1990. Development of a wetland conservation and development programme for Tanzania. IUCN, Gland, Switzerland. 113 pp.

Omari, C.K. 1990. Traditional African land ethics. Pages 167-175. In: J.R. Engel and J.G. Engel (Eds). *Ethics of Environment and Development: Global Challenge and International Response*. Belhaven Press, London.

Omari, C.K. 1991. A short report on the future of Lower Moshi Irrigation Project. Unpublished report submitted to Japanese International Cooperation Agency.

Swantz, L.M. 1985. *Women in Development: A Creative Role Denied? The Case of Tanzania.* G. Hurse and Company, London. 177 pp.

Temple, P. 1975. Geology. Pages 42-43. In: L. Berry (Ed.). *Tanzania in Maps.* University of London Press, London.

United Republic of Tanzania (URT). 1967. *Atlas of Tanzania.* URT, Dar es Salaam.

River basin planning and management of wetlands

F.J. Manongi

Rufiji Basin Development Authority
P.O. Box 9320
Dar es Salaam

Summary

The Rufiji River basin has wetlands with economic functions that require conservation; these functions have hitherto been taken for granted. Mismanagement of this basin would have direct effects on these various functions and their values. The execution of large projects (e.g. hydropower and irrigation) may have effects which need to be evaluated. Coordinated planning and management at the river basin level is required for the sustainable utilisation of wetlands.

Introduction

To illustrate river basin planning, the catchment of the Rufiji River has been used as an example in this paper. The Rufiji Basin (Figure 1) is the largest catchment basin in Tanzania, covering 177,420 km^2, and has the highest potential for hydropower in Tanzania.

The Rufiji Basin Development Authority (RUBADA) was established in 1975 by an Act of Parliament. Its primary functions are the generation of electricity by hydroworks, the undertaking of flood control measures, and the promotion and regulation of activities in the sectors of industry, agriculture, forestry, fisheries, tourism and transport. Since RUBADA's establishment, its major activities have been in the research and planning of the energy sector.

The planning of the Stiegler's Gorge Hydropower Project was developed to tendering level but, unfortunately, the project was not implemented due to the high costs involved. A pre-feasibility study, carried out by RUBADA on irrigated agriculture in the Lower Rufiji, recommended wetland rice as the main crop for both large scale and small scale irrigation. RUBADA has two irrigation projects in the Rufiji Basin; KOTACO, in the Kilombero Valley, and TAN/IRAN IKARUDEP, in the Lower Rufiji Valley. These are being executed in collaboration with the Governments of Korea and Iran respectively.

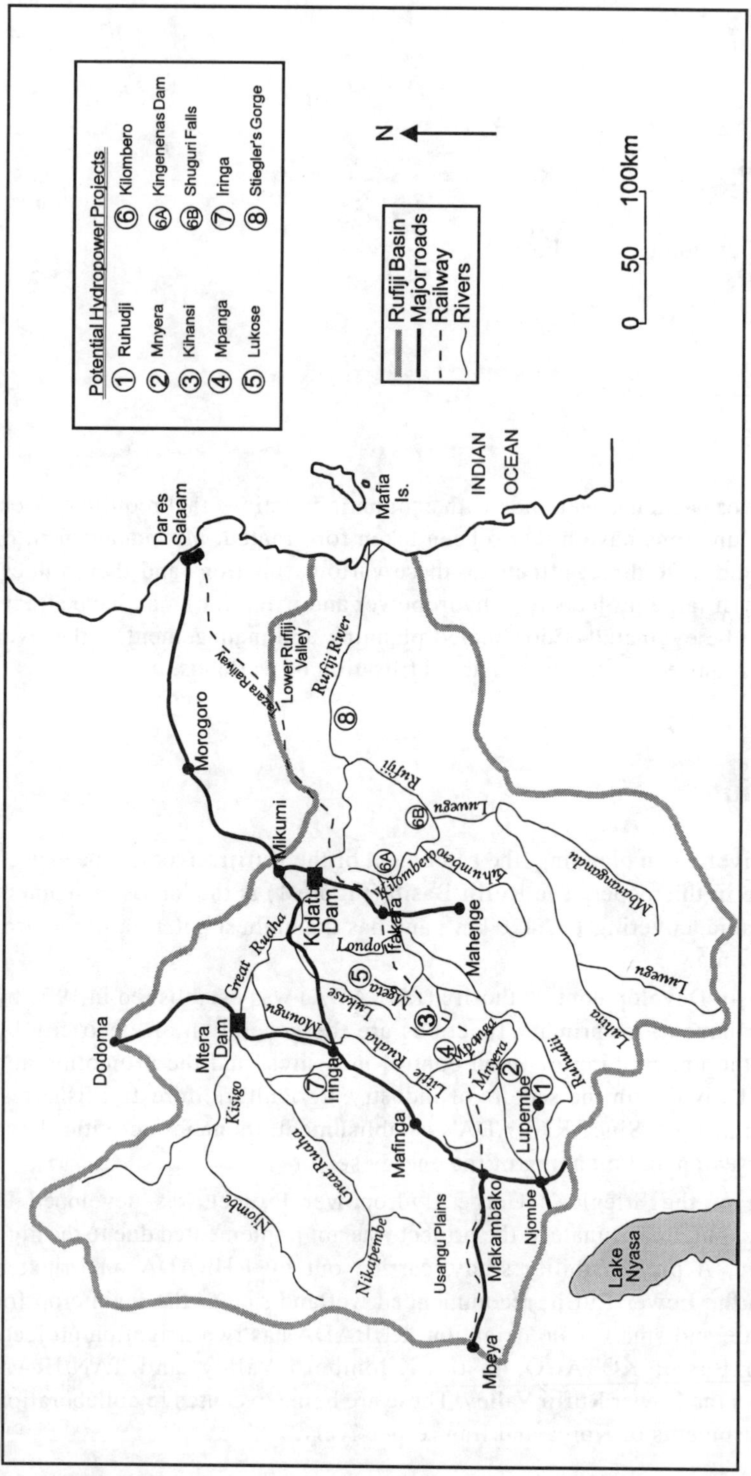

Figure 1   Rufiji Basin showing hydropower potential

The importance of wetlands

Wetlands are important resources which include freshwater swamps, floodplains (Kilombero and Rufiji Rivers), coastal swamps and mangroves (Rufiji Delta).

The Selous Game Reserve, within the Rufiji Basin, covers 21,000 km^2 and is one of the largest game reserves in Africa with approximately 750,000 large mammals. The wetlands therein provide habitats for a wide range of animals. If communication is improved, the Selous Game Reserve offers an alternative environment for tourists compared with the commercialised tourism of the northern circuit. Hitherto, most of the tourist activities have been concentrated in the northern circuit but there are now plans to include the Selous Game Reserve in beach and safari holiday packages. It should be emphasised that one of RUBADA's functions is to promote tourism.

The total mangrove area of Tanzania is approximately 50,000 ha, of which 32,000 ha are concentrated in the Rufiji Delta. Mangroves are harvested mainly for export to the Gulf States. There is a need to conserve the mangroves and minimise the destruction of the resource by non-sustainable activities.

The importance of wetlands can be further appreciated when the floodplains are taken into account. Tanzania is a net importer of food and these areas are potential 'bread baskets' for the country. However, floodplains experience both flooding and drought, and agricultural developments, especially in the Lower Rufiji Valley, must address these related but diverse problems.

Wetlands are also the sites of rich fisheries and professional fishermen depend on these areas. Some farmers become fishermen at certain times of the year when they fish for home consumption and for sale.

Wetlands of the Rufiji River basin

The Rufiji River basin covers 20% of the area of Tanzania, has 10% of Tanzania's population and 30% of its surface water. The basin can be conveniently divided into three parts, the Lower Rufiji Valley, the Kilombero Valley and the Usangu Plains.

The Lower Rufiji Valley

In the Lower Rufiji Valley, 114,000 ha of land were identified as suitable for irrigation, of which 57,000 ha were highly suitable for irrigated agriculture (especially rice production). Some 33,000 ha were rated as moderately suitable and the balance of 24,000 ha, mostly in the delta, was marginally suitable due to potential salinity problems.

In the Lower Rufiji floodplain there are a number of small, permanent or temporary, lacustrine ecosystems (Figure 2). Three of the main lakes are situated south

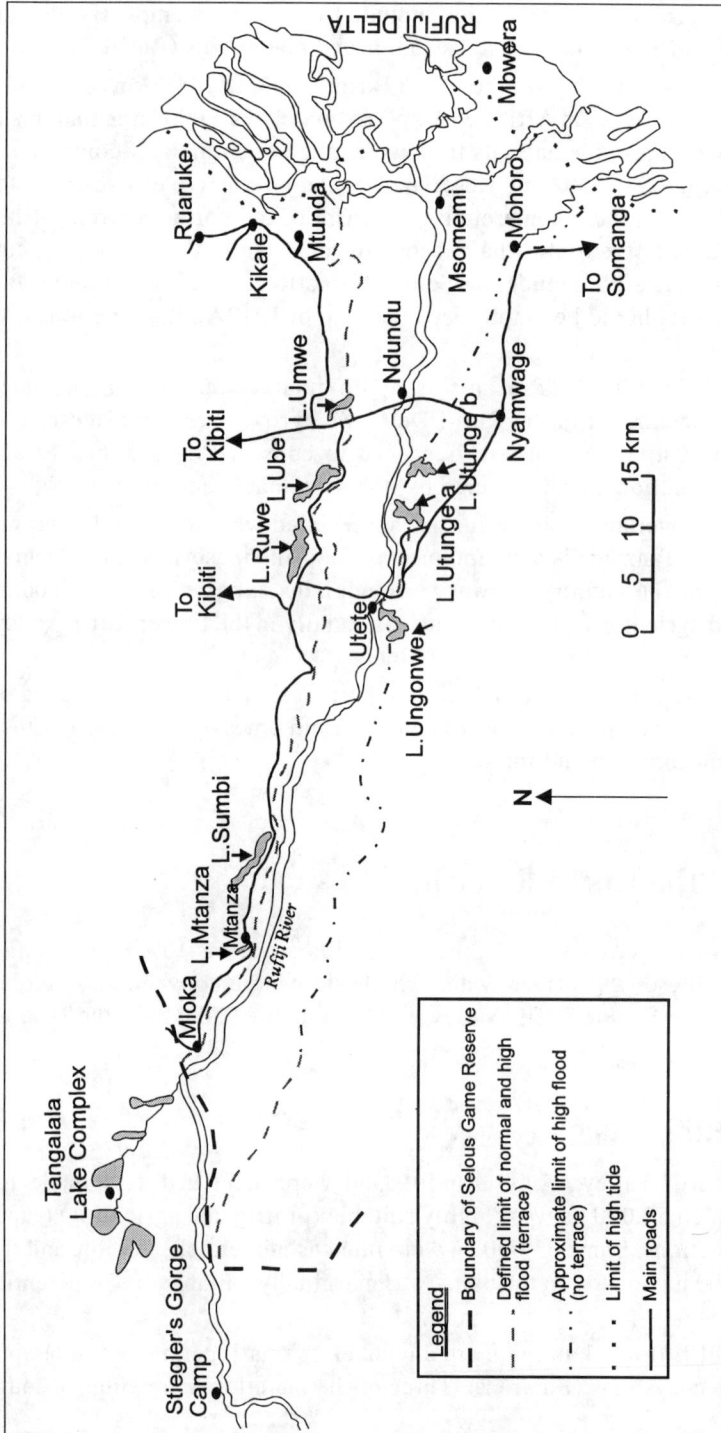

Figure 2   Lower Rufiji Valley and floodplain showing lacustrine wetlands and the delta

of the river and ten lakes lie to the north of which five belong to the Tangalala lacustrine wetlands.

Within the Rufiji Delta are found marine sediments of the Jurassic and Cretaceous periods. These are overlain by recent alluvial deposits (mainly sand, silt and clay) transported from the Rufiji Basin as suspended sediment in rivers. Deposition of this sediment produces a deltaic region of shifting river channels where the Rufiji River distributaries fan out from a line drawn between Kikale in the north and Mohoro in the south (Figure 2). The water level in the channels is affected by ocean tides. A substantial mangrove forest (320 km^2) has developed, making the Rufiji Delta one of the largest compact mangrove areas on the east coast of Africa.

The Kilombero Valley

Approximately 38,750 ha of the Kilombero Valley (Figure 1) were designated to be suitable for irrigated agriculture. The majority (60%) of the Kilombero Valley is prone to flooding. Floods can be controlled by constructing protection banks on both sides of a cultivated area and arable land can be drained by ditches running down the slopes to remove excess water into the flood zones. The Kibasira Swamp is found on the Kilombero River.

The Usangu Plains

The Usangu Plains are extensive alluvial plains located to the northeast of Mbeya town (Figure 1). They cover 1.5 million ha of which 208,000 ha are considered irrigable. In the Usangu Plains are wetlands known as Utengule Swamps.

River basin planning

River basin planning must be carried out within overall national objectives such as self sufficiency in food production. Projects can be planned on the basis of existing natural resources (such as land, hydropower and forests) but unsustainable exploitation of resources can lead to serious problems. The costs and benefits of exploiting a resource must be determined before implementation because projects may also have negative impacts. A simple and commonly used rule in project assessment is that the total (overall) benefits should always exceed the costs. Economists usually speak of a project cycle which means the various stages of gathering data and decision making between the project's inception and completion. To illustrate some of these stages, examples from RUBADA's activities will be used.

Project identification

Project identification is usually based on the existence of a certain resource and/or as the result of an existing problem. As the prices of fossil fuels increased steadily from 1973, many governments, including Tanzania, looked towards cheaper sources of power, such as hydroelectricity. In the Rufiji Basin, there is an estimated hydropower potential of approximately 3,700 megawatts.

Because of food shortages in Tanzania, it was necessary to utilise the abundant land resource in the Rufiji Basin which has soils suitable for crop production. The KOTACO rice project arose from this line of thinking.

RUBADA has identified a problem of watershed mismanagement of the Rufiji River at Usangu Plains and therefore has initiated a project to redress the situation.

Pre-feasibility study

At pre-feasibility level, some rough projections and costs are made but further work will be needed to determine whether the project is viable. At this stage a team of specialists (engineers, agriculturalists, agronomists, economists, environmentalists, sociologists), covering a wide range of disciplines, work together.

RUBADA engaged Agrar- und Hydrotechnik GmbH (AHT) to do a pre-feasibility study on irrigated agricultural development in the Lower Rufiji Valley. AHT recommended a large scale irrigation project of 65,000 ha, divided into 9 blocks (RUBADA, 1980). Ikwiriri block (15,500 ha) was recommended for initial development because of its superior soils and accessibility. Due to the high cost, complications and environmental problems of large scale irrigation projects, RUBADA has recommended a study of small scale irrigation projects.

Also at pre-feasibility level, RUBADA had commissioned the Ardhi Institute to produce the Usangu Land Use Plan. The consultants have collected data on the existing situation in the Usangu Plains, detailed trends in development, and identified areas of conflict. This study could not be continued due to lack of funds.

Feasibility study

At the feasibility study stage, the economist narrows down the range of project options to the few that are most promising and recommends appropriate projects and courses of action. For the Stiegler's Gorge Project, a large hydropower project, a wide ranging study was carried out on the multi-sectoral development of the Lower Rufiji Basin, including the impact of the project on the development potential of agriculture, fisheries, forestry and tourism in the area. In addition, a series of environmental studies were commissioned which focussed on ecological and demographic impacts and covered wildlife, water quality, vegetation clearance, human settlements and health problems.

Aspects of river basin projects

Projects in the Rufiji River basin involve the sectors of energy, agriculture, forestry, fisheries and watershed management. The projects must be evaluated to ensure the environmentally sound management of water resources. In general, a good project has the following attributes:

1. The resource itself is maintained and adverse effects on other resources are considered and, where possible, reduced. The development should be self sustaining and other resources, for example wetlands which have certain ecological functions, are maintained or effects on them minimised.

2. Options for future development are not foreclosed. This is important because some actions are irreversible.

3. Efficiency in the use of water and capital are key criteria in strategy selection.

All projects require monitoring and evaluation. Monitoring is surveillance over the implementation period of the project to ensure that work schedules, inputs, targeted outputs and other required actions are progressing according to the plan. Evaluation determines, systematically and objectively, the impact, effectiveness and relevance of project activities. It ensures that the project objectives are met and that lessons learned are used to rectify problems or to assist in the design and management of similar projects.

Hydropower

Hydropower projects do not have a major impact on environment. The summary of the environmental impacts of smaller hydropower projects, identified by RUBADA Consultants, is shown in Table 1. Besides the provision of inexpensive power, hydropower projects make a significant contribution to the fishery resource, have little impact on tourism and may improve the agricultural potential in some areas.

Agriculture

The Rufiji Basin has a high potential for irrigated agriculture. A number of large irrigation projects, growing sugar and rice, are operating in the Kilombero Valley and Usangu Plains. Other projects, such as KOTACO, are still in the construction stage.

Forestry

There are 92 forest reserves in the Rufiji Basin, covering approximately 10% of the total basin area. These forests are very important for the regulation of water resources. Unsustainable forest exploitation or clearance leads to reduction in quality and quantity of water resources. While there is awareness of the need to protect water sources, there are not enough financial and manpower resources to effect that protection.

The Rufiji Basin has suitable areas for industrial plantation forests. Afforestation has taken place in the highlands using exotic pines and cypress. RUBADA does not have the financial resources for afforestation at either industrial plantation or village level.

Table 1   Summary of impacts of smaller hydropower projects in the Rufiji Basin

Project	Settlements	Infrastructure	Agriculture	Health	Fisheries	Wildlife/tourism
Ruhudji	Minor resettlement may be necessary	Some relocation	Minor	Minor	None	None
Mnyera	Some resettlement may be necessary	Road access to Taveta may be cut. Alternative route *via* dam wall must be provided	Minor	Minor, but control measures may be necessary	Minor	None
Kihansi	None	Minor	Minor	Minor	None	Minor
Mpanga	None	None	None	None	None	None
Lukose	Some resettlement may be necessary	Some road relocation may be necessary	Minor	Minor, but control measures necessary due to high population	None	Minor
Kingenenas	Some effects of inundation on settlements. Measures must be taken to protect Ifakara from flooding	Ifakara-Mahenge ferry service terminated. Alternative route *via* dam wall must be provided	40,000 ha farmland submerged, leading to resettlement of 10,000 people	Severe adverse affects on Ifakara unless control measures initiated	No negative impact on commercial fisheries	Minor impact on present hunting areas. Control of poaching will be necessary
Shuguri Falls	None	None	None	Measures necessary to protect construction and operating staff	None	Minor impact on present hunting areas. Control of poaching will be necessary
Iringa	Major resettlement	Considerable impact on Tanzam highway, 220kV power system, Tazara pipeline and local roads	Considerable loss of land leading to extensive resettlement	Adverse impacts will be considerable due to high population	Minor	None

Fisheries

During the flood period, oxygen rich water spreads over vegetation. Fish move into the shallow water of floodplains to feed on the masses of insects, worms, decaying plants, fallen fruits and mineralised water; during this time they breed.

One of the RUBADA's main activities is to institute measures of flood control, therefore, a thorough appraisal of the effect of this on fisheries needs to be carried out. Limnological studies, carried out along the Rufiji system as far as the delta and Mafia Channel, show that the whole Rufiji system has commercial fishery potential.

Water resource management

Hydrological studies in the Rufiji Basin are necessary to determine the availability of surface water resources for human consumption, livestock use, irrigation and hydropower generation. Planned, sustainable use of this resource must take into consideration various existing and potential conflicts in the exploitation of the water resource of the Rufiji Basin.

Comprehensive management planning of water resources

Water projects are usually conceived as a result of existing or potential problems and have a specific objective to achieve. In this world of scarce resources, and as environmental considerations gain ground, alternatives must be appraised and their implications and impacts assessed.

To ensure optimal utilisation of the water resource, it must be treated as an economic good and economists must make cost/benefit analyses for water projects. It is not easy or possible to quantify all aspects of a project. Water resources have numerous potential uses, some of which compete with each other. This problem has already been identified in the Rufiji River basin.

The best use of the water resource occurs when water using activities are coordinated and planned together. The numerous water uses for the Rufiji system include hydropower generation (Kidatu and Mtera Dams), flood control (planned for the Lower Rufiji Valley) and irrigation development (Kilombero and Rufiji Valleys). It is necessary to integrate water planning with overall economic and social planning. Hydropower and irrigation projects are usually expensive and therefore must be in line with the economic and social conditions existing in the country.

Water resource development affects other resources, for instance wetlands, and there is need for coordination between agencies representing all aspects of water resource development. An obvious coordinating agency would be a river basin development authority. To ensure orderly and sustainable development, such an authority must have the powers to plan, monitor and control project activities taking place in the basin. The authority should also be empowered to make and enforce by-laws relating to the management of the river basin.

Public participation

Public participation in river basin management has been taken for granted and there are cases where conservation programmes have been unsuccessful because of the peoples' non-involvement. Public involvement should ideally take place as early as possible in the project.

Environmental effects of basin projects

Until very recently, most third world countries did not give sustainable development its due weight. RUBADA now emphasises the use of Environmental Impact Assessments (EIAs) but it must have the financial means to commission them. In developed countries, different interest and pressure groups are consulted and involved in EIAs.

Social impacts

Apart from the economic and environmental dimensions, projects have social impacts. Usually people's traditional life styles are modified as a result of large projects in their area. New towns arise and lifestyles become more urban; new economic activities begin while others are abandoned. Often products that used to be produced within the locality have to be imported.

Afforestation

Water resources management essentially means watershed management. Therefore, RUBADA must encourage better land use practices in the basin. Afforestation programmes must be financed by the government and donors, as private investors will be discouraged by the long gestation period of the project. For successful afforestation projects, the villagers must be mobilised and involved at the planning stage.

Conclusion

River basins contain many resources and if these resources are not exploited in an orderly way the ecological balance will be disturbed. Within the basin, it is possible to find experts giving contradicting advice and their work needs to be integrated and coordinated by one body, such as RUBADA.

The exploitation of resources is part of development. Attempts must be made to replace resources and to conserve those that cannot be replenished. Projects should be appraised for their impacts on the whole basin.

Comprehensive data should be collected on the resources of the basin and project impacts can only be determined if this data is accurate. RUBADA needs financial and technical support to carry out these functions properly. RUBADA further needs to have legal powers over the basin area in order to plan, monitor and control development activities within the basin.

Bibliography

Haule, A.I.A. 1981. Conservation aspects and resource utilization in the Rufiji Basin. RUBADA. Unpublished report.

Haule, A.I.A. 1982. State of water resources and wildlife conservation. RUBADA. Unpublished report.

Irvin, G. 1978. *Modern Cost-Benefit Methods. An Introduction to Financial, Economic, and Social Appraisal of Development Projects.* McMillan Press, London.

RUBADA. 1980. Rufiji multipurpose development: Identification study on ecological impacts of the Stiegler's Gorge Project. Report prepared by Agrar- und Hydrotechnik (AHT), West Germany.

RUBADA. 1982. Stiegler's Gorge Multipurpose Development Project. Unpublished report. Stokes Kennedy Cowley Management Consultants, Dublin, Ireland.

RUBADA. 1983. Lower Rufiji Valley integration study. Unpublished report. Norplan, Oslo, Norway.

RUBADA. 1984. The Basin Hydropower Master Plan. Unpublished report. Norconsult, Norway.

Thanh, N.C. and A. Biswas (Eds). 1990. *Environmentally Sound Management of Water Resources.* Oxford University Press. UK.

Management of the Rufiji Delta as a wetland

R.B.B. Mwalyosi

Institute of Resource Assessment
University of Dar es Salaam
P.O. Box 35097
Dar es Salaam

Summary

The complex system of marine and freshwater ecosystems, and wetland resources, is described for the Rufiji Delta, an area of over 53,000 ha. Multiple resource use and the risk of overexploitation are mentioned together with the effects of up-stream developments on the delta ecosystems. Possibilities for an integrated resource management system are outlined, including a zoning plan for utilisation of the mangroves.

Introduction

The Rufiji Delta covers 53,255 ha (Semesi, 1989) and forms part of the Rufiji River basin which extends for some 177,000 km^2 (RUBADA, 1981a) (Figure 1). As a result of deposition of sediment carried by the Rufiji River towards the coast, the shoreline has shifted seaward and presently protrudes some 15 km into the Mafia Channel. The north- south extent of the delta is 65 km and its depth inland is approximately 23 km (Figure 2).

The delta is traversed by numerous deltaic branches of the Rufiji River, of which nine are major. At present, the activity of the four northern channels is increasing, while that of the southern ones is decreasing. The tides travel up these branches over considerable distances, particularly when the Rufiji is low, and may penetrate as far as the village of Msomemi (25 km inland as the crow flies, see Figure 2). During floods, silt laden Rufiji waters penetrate far into the delta and deposit river sediments, especially along the most active deltaic branches.

The estuary and delta of the Rufiji River seem to be in a state of dynamic equilibrium. The geometry and the course of the several tidal branches changes continuously by sediment deposition and erosion. The morphological conditions are disturbed by changing hydraulic features, such as fluctuating discharges, varying intrusion of salinity, and changes in sediment transport.

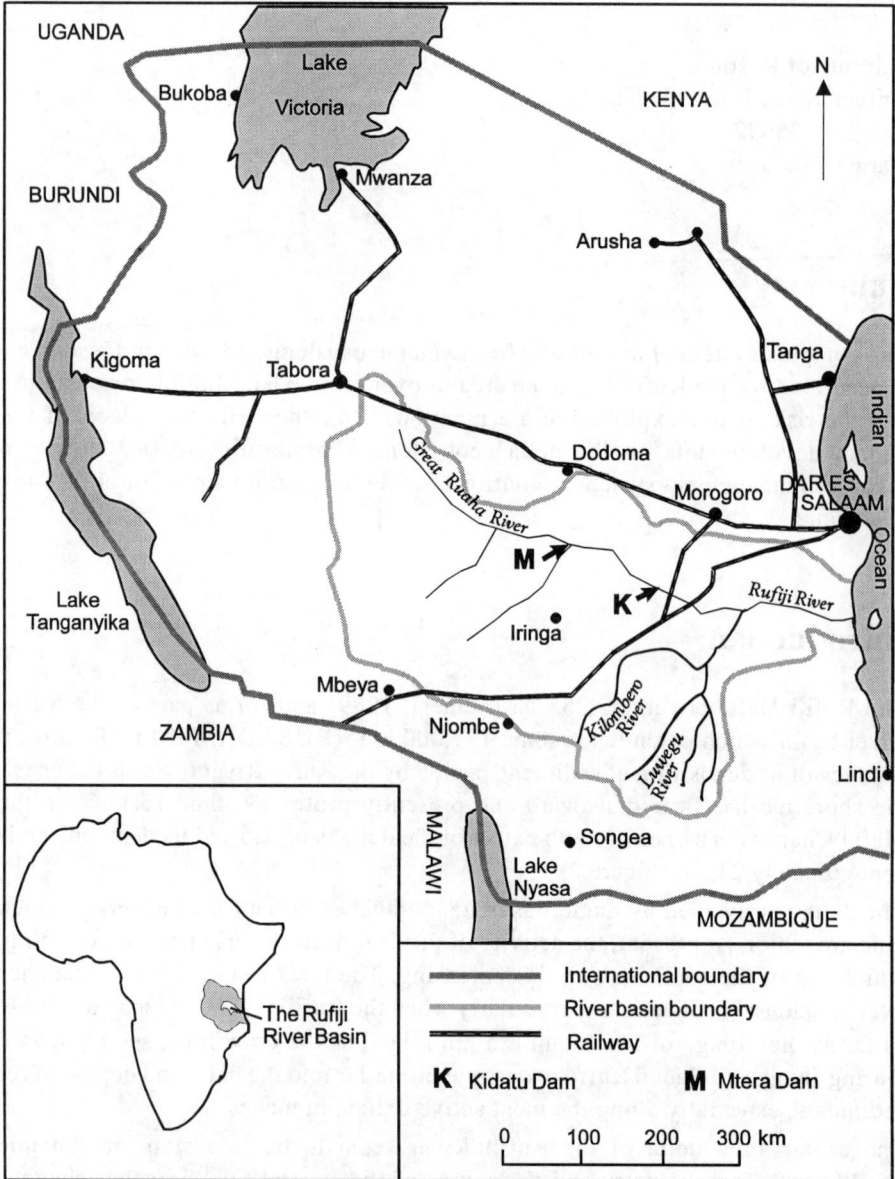

Figure 1   Location of the Rufiji River basin

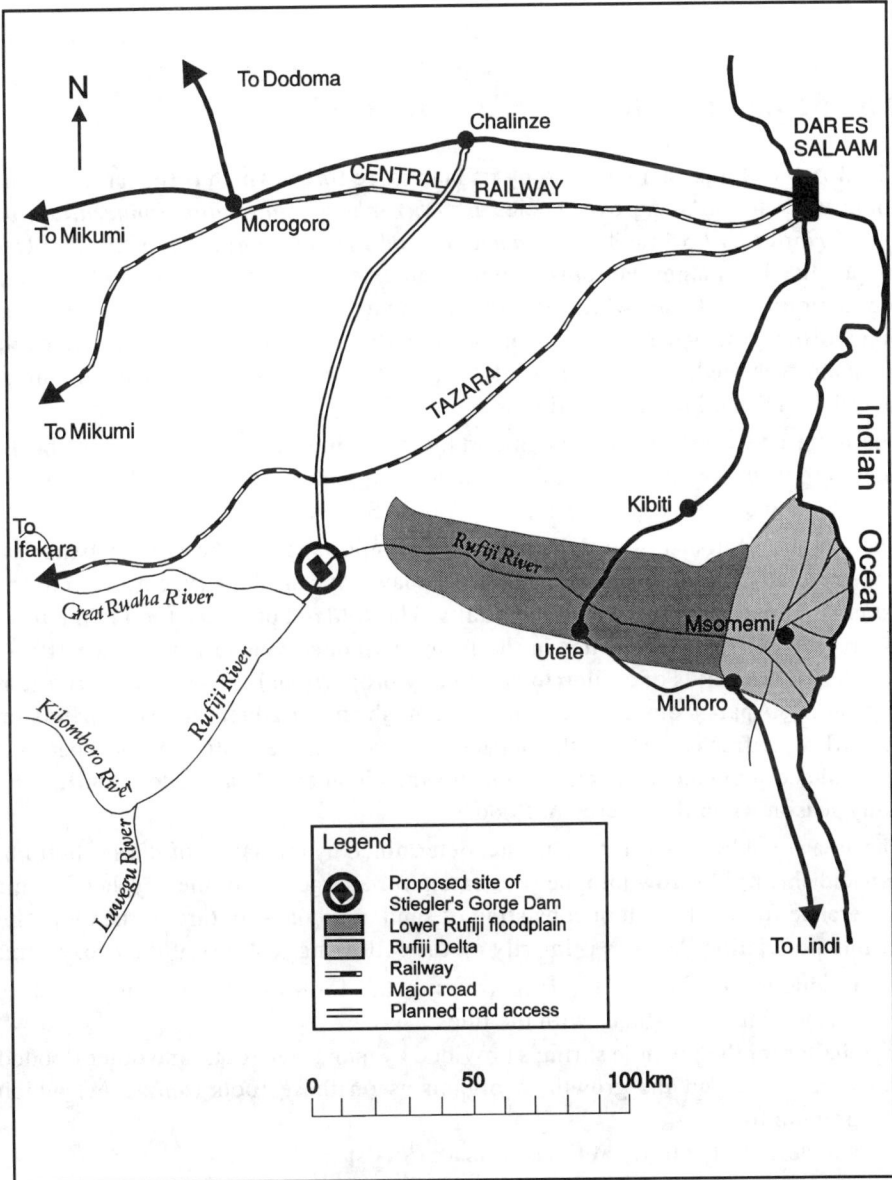

Figure 2   Map showing the location of the Rufiji Delta and floodplain

Mangroves are a common feature of the delta. They are adapted to soils without oxygen and many have pneumatophores (breathing roots). The high osmotic pressure in their tissues allows them to resist changes in salinity. Mangrove areas are unstable as rivers deposit alluvium to form mudflats while, concurrently, the sea causes erosion. By the use of stilt roots, mangroves are able to withstand such soil mobility.

The deltaic resources

The Rufiji Delta is characterised by its mangrove forest which is the largest in the country. Common mangrove species are *Rhizophora mucronata*, *Sonneratia alba* and *Ceriops tagal*, while *Avicennia marina* and *Bruguiera gymnorrhiza* occur less frequently. The mangrove forest supports an extensive food web through its high production of detritus which is broken down by fungi and bacteria. Several omnivorous crustaceans of commercial importance spend part of their life cycle in mangroves feeding on the detritus, live benthic microalgae, occasional animal material and fine inorganic particles.

The delta and Mafia Island are important wintering grounds for migrant birds, including waders and terns. Wildlife, such as hippopotamus, crocodiles and monkeys, feed and shelter in the mangrove forest (Semesi, 1989).

The aquatic system in the delta is of great importance to the shrimp fisheries. Commercially important penaeid shrimps spawn at sea; the larvae move into the estuary and return to the sea as sub-adults. The wetland provides food in the form of organic detritus and shelter in the form of flooded vegetation. Turner (1977) has shown the yields of shrimp to be directly proportional to the area of intertidal vegetation. Apart from the estuarine system, shrimp production also depends on the inflow of freshwater and the nutrients thus discharged into the sea. The most pronounced movement of freshwater into the channels of the delta is during the rainy season when the river is in flood.

The area suitable for shrimps is further determined by the nature of the sea bottom. Penaeid shrimps burrow into the substratum for a large part of the day, hence their preference for a soft bottom consisting of sand, mud or a mixture of the two. The shrimp population depends primarily on the following features of the ecosystem:

- production of food in the mangroves in the form of organic litter which is flushed into the estuary with the tides;
- shelter for the juvenile shrimps provided by mangrove roots, and other flooded vegetation, and the growth of organisms on these roots (*aufwuchs*) which provide food;
- a lowering of salinity at times of peak floods;
- deposition of riverine sediment on the sea bottom;
- inflow of nutrients carried by the river to the sea.

Resource utilisation

The Rufiji Delta mangrove forest is heavily exploited for both the export market and local use. Mangrove poles from the Rufiji Delta have been traded since ancient times for house and boat building; an export market has long existed in the Arabian Peninsular and Gulf States. The poles ('boriti') of the Rufiji Delta are held in high esteem due to their diameter and shape. Other traditional uses of mangroves include fish traps, fish net floats, animal fodder and ropes (Mainoya, 1986; Semesi, 1989). Mangroves are also being degraded through conversion to single use options, such as farming, salt evaporation, lime making, firewood and charcoal production. The Rufiji Delta mangroves are cleared for rice farming which is carried out from December to June; the yields vary from 12 to 50 bags/ha. Farmers cultivate plots continuously for approximately 7 years, after which time they abandon them to clear new farms (Semesi, 1989).

The fishing industry in the delta supports more than 200 fishermen. No statistics are available on the species composition of fish and crustaceans caught in the delta. However, the current commercial prawn catch consists of *Penaeus indicus, P. monodon*, and *Metapenaeus monoceros*. At present, over 80% of all prawns caught in Tanzania come from the Rufiji Delta and the area northwards along the shoreline to Kisiju. Over 90% of the prawns caught are exported. Current production from the Rufiji Delta is unknown but the potential catch is approximately 7,000 t/year for prawns and 10,000 t/year for fish (RUBADA, 1981b).

The artisanal fishery depends largely on the mass emigration of sub-adults from the estuary. Individual fishermen use hand or cast nets to collect prawns from shallow mangrove channels or groups of fishermen work together and harvest prawns caught in 'uzi', large funnel shaped traps staked in (or just below) the inter-tidal zone. Only the local people fish in the delta while commercial trawlers tend to exploit the adult spawning grounds and carry out most of their work in 6-20 m of water (Dorsey, 1979). Although prawns are currently the most important of the commercially exploited mangrove Crustacea, there are two species of large crabs which have high fishery potential. Both these crabs, *Portunus pelagicus* and *Scylla serrata* remain virtually unexploited. Like prawns, they are intimately linked to the protected waters of the estuaries and mangrove swamp.

Most of the fish are caught by artisanal fishermen who sell the smoked product in major towns, especially Dar es Salaam. The marketing of fish and prawns from the Rufiji Delta is well organised and is largely controlled by businessmen from Dar es Salaam who provide boats, engines, cooling facilities and transport to the city.

Potential environmental impacts on the Rufiji Delta

Upstream damming

Increased damming in the catchment area would lead to regulated discharges through the estuary such that there would be relatively less flow during the flood season and greater flow during the dry season.

Salinity intrusion

In the normal situation, low river flows occur for a limited time (several months) and the increased salinity during this period is then flushed out by the high flows of the rainy season. Damming of the river in the upstream areas may lead to above average flows; as a result, the higher dry season flows may push the salt wedge further seaward, while in the rainy season, the flushing and leaching effect would be reduced. The overall impact would be decreased variation of salt intrusion over the year. At the sea side of the delta, average salinity would increase, probably affecting the overall ecology of the delta. Deforestation, overgrazing and extensive rural activities in the catchment area may have similar effects on the delta ecology by altering runoff and hence increasing river flows.

Morphological changes

In the short term, no significant morphological changes are expected from damming in the upstream areas, as the river would pick up sediments downstream until its transport capacity is fulfilled. However, in the long run, the sediment supply to the delta would decrease substantially; delta formation would cease and coastal erosion along the Mafia Channel, as well as deepening of the tidal channels, could occur.

Reduction in sediment supply to the estuary and delta would not only enhance the growth of coral reefs, thus rendering the area unsuitable for prawn trawling, but would also lead to a reduction in areas of suitable prawn habitat.

Results of changes in the flood regime

Land use changes in the catchment area may lead to changes in the climatic regime of the area and may also affect the flooding regime. Relatively higher discharges during the dry season would lead to the conversion of some mangrove areas into reeds.

The prawn, *Metapenaeus monoceros* migrates out of the delta to the adult feeding grounds with the short rains, in response to increased discharges. *Penaeus indicus* and *P. monodon* usually require higher discharge levels to stimulate them into emigration. Any changes in the river flow regime may interfere with the synchrony of the adult feeding and spawning cycles and thus lead to reduced prawn production.

The crab, *Scylla serrata* is particularly sensitive to low salinity estuarine waters. It emigrates from the estuary with the onset of the rainy season and would be sensitive to any change in the flooding pattern of the river.

Fish, such as *Hilsa kelee* and *Liza macrolepis*, spawn at the beginning of the early rains and would also be affected should there be significant change in the flooding regime.

Pollution

The presence of biocides, drained from agricultural areas, may be harmful to both flora and fauna of the delta. According to Semesi (1989), DDT application on farms leads to the death of non-target animals including fish and prawns. The increasing industrialisation (the Mufundi Pulp and Paper Mill, Sao Hill Forest Project) and application of agricultural chemicals in the catchment area will increase the level of nutrients and/or toxins in the estuarine water and affect the ecology of the delta.

Resource overexploitation

On the basis of the positive relationship between mangrove areas and prawn production, extensive reduction of mangrove area would lead to a reduction in prawn production. Moreover, mangroves are endemic to very few coastal areas and substantial harvesting of this resource may lead to the disappearance of some species and thus decreased biodiversity. Although most of the local people utilise the mangrove resources sustainably, it is the commercial activities which are a major threat to the resource. However, shifting cultivation practices by the local people encourage the replacement of mangroves by sedges (Semesi, 1989).

Management of the Rufiji Delta

River basin uses and their effects on the delta's ecology

The Rufiji Basin is very rich in resources and significant potential exists for both irrigated and rainfed agriculture. Over 622,400 ha are suitable for irrigation (RUBADA, 1981a), of which more than 10,000 ha have been developed. Iringa and Mbeya, both within the Rufiji Basin, are two of the four major grain producing regions in Tanzania. Increased grain production in these areas is mainly through expansion and intensification of smallholder farming. Haphazard agricultural development in the catchment may have a significant impact on the delta's ecology.

Tanzania's energy policy is designed to meet all energy needs, as far as possible, through development of indigenous resources, especially hydropower (Mwalyosi, 1988). The Rufiji Basin contains over 60% of the hydropower potential in Tanzania. Apart from the developed sites at Mtera and Kidatu, the other major potential sites include Stiegler's Gorge, Kihansi, Ikondo and Ruhudji. Therefore, development of hydropower in the Rufiji Basin is important and justifiable but such developments and related activities will invariably affect the ecology of the delta.

The human population of the basin (more than 16% of Tanzania's population) is increasing and, associated with this, the demand for land resources is rising as well. In recent years, Iringa and Mbeya have received many pastoral migrants from the northern parts of the country where rangelands have been reduced and over-grazed. As the population increases in these regions, resource utilisation will be intensified and land degradation, especially through soil erosion, is likely to increase. This would affect the silt and freshwater supply to the delta.

During the last three decades, several public works such as the Tanzam highway, the Tazara railway, the Makambako-Songea highway, and hydropower develop-ment on the Great Ruaha River have set the stage for rapid exploitation of the basin's resources. In the Mafia Channel, prospecting for petroleum is still in progress. The great potential for fisheries in the delta and Mafia Channel has attracted many local and foreign fishing companies to the area. These activities, unless properly planned and coordinated, may lead to resource degradation in the delta.

The basin has abundant, undeveloped wildlife resources, with spectacular tourist attractions in the Selous and Rungwa Game Reserves, and Mikumi and Ruaha National Parks. The Rufiji River is navigable by boat from Kidai downstream to the Indian Ocean; connections can be made, by boat, to Mafia Island and Dar es Salaam. The present government priority is to develop the tourist potential in the southern part of the country in an effort to reduce the current tourist pressure on the northern circuit. Uncontrolled tourist traffic through the delta and/or the Mafia Channel may affect the estuary through pollution and overfishing.

Integrated resource management

An integrated resource management approach is needed for the whole Rufiji Basin, delta and coastal waters. A single authority, the Rufiji Basin Development Author-ity (RUBADA), was established in 1975 to coordinate and regulate the utilisation of resources in the basin. Since its establishment, however, RUBADA has concen-trated on promoting resource development, mainly in the Kilombero and Lower Rufiji Valleys. Very little, if any, attention has been paid to the management of the basin as a whole. By regulation, RUBADA has powers to:

1. Regulate access to any part of the basin by unauthorised persons or institutions.
2. Regulate the use of waters.
3. Minimise pollution of waters.
4. Provide safety standards for persons and institutions implementing hydro-electric and other works.

The responsibility of promotion and regulation requires RUBADA to have a Land and Water Use Master Plan for the whole basin including the Rufiji Delta. To eliminate or minimise environmental hazards as well as conflicts among projects competing for similar resources, RUBADA ensures that environmental impact assessments are carried out for all development projects.

Watershed research programme

The management of the Rufiji Delta should be made in the context of its dependence on the land use of the adjacent catchment and its inter-relationships with estuaries, lagoons, coral reefs and the Mafia Channel.

Catchment basin management should be concerned with the establishment of management control over precipitation water. Although much of the hydrologic cycle is beyond management control, the goal should be to provide practical and acceptable means to reduce erosion and surface runoff. Most current conservation programmes for controlling watershed problems are developed and tested in temperate regions of the developed world. Although the general principles of watershed management are straightforward, their application and adaptation to local conditions depends, in a large part, on characteristics of local climate, soils and hydrology; such data have yet to be fully quantified for Tanzania. Technical research that is highly applied and problem orientated is the key to developing more productive and sustained uses of soil and water resources in the whole Rufiji System. A thorough research programme would be many faceted and involve the following activities:

1. Resource surveys to ascertain problems.

2. Land evaluations based on natural resource surveys. This would help to summarise basic resource information in ways that are understandable to all those involved with management of land and water resources. Land evaluations can integrate resource inventory data with economic parameters to aid land owners, managers and policy makers in making decisions about resource use.

3. A major component of watershed research should be devoted to adaptive research, a new concept which takes advantage of information already available and adapts management techniques to local conditions. Ideally, an adaptive research programme would involve a variety of organisations, public agencies, extension workers and land users in order to minimise costs.

4. Watershed development projects would benefit from monitoring the impacts of project activities on water and soil resources. Such monitoring would necessitate the involvement of researchers from many disciplines.

5. The educational needs of the different groups involved in watershed use needs to be addressed. Such groups include land users, extension workers, managers, policy makers, the general public and the scientific community.

Proposed management programme for the Rufiji Delta

The management of the Rufiji Delta should take into consideration the economic, biological, ecological, educational and aesthetic importance of its resources at the local, national and international level. Any management programme for mangrove resources should take account of the needs and interests of the local communities.

The proposed management programme divides the mangroves of the Rufiji Delta into the following four utilisation zones (Semesi, 1989):

ZONE I: Total protection forests
ZONE II: Productive forests
ZONE III: Forests requiring recovery
ZONE IV: Development areas

The area is stratified in such a way that different activities are permitted in different zones to strike a balance between development and conservation, thus ensuring sustainable use of the resources.

Bibliography

Dorsey, K.T. 1979. Report on the prawn fisheries of the Rufiji delta with particular reference to possible changes resulting from modifications to the environment by the proposed dam at Stiegler's Gorge. FAO, Rome. FAO/TCP/URT/8806. Technical Paper No. 2. 53 pp.

Mainoya, J.R. 1986. The use of mangroves and their products by the local community in Tanzania. Pages 37-48. In: J.R. Mainoya and P.R. Siegel (Eds). *Status and Utilization of Mangroves. Proceeding of a workshop on 'Save the Mangrove Ecosystems in Tanzania'*. 21-22 February 1986, Dar es Salaam. University of Dar es Salaam.

Mwalyosi, R.B.B. 1988. Environmental impacts of the proposed Stiegler's Gorge hydropower project, Tanzania. *Environmental Conservation* 15(3):250-254.

RUBADA (Rufiji Basin Development Authority). 1981a. Promotion and regulation of development activities in the Rufiji basin. Unpublished report.

RUBADA (Rufiji Basin Development Authority). 1981b. Study of the impact of the Stiegler's Gorge multipurpose project on fisheries in the Rufiji delta and Mafia Channel. Final report by Atkins Land and Water Management, Cambridge, UK.

Semesi, A.K. 1989. The mangrove resources of the Rufiji delta, Tanzania. Paper presented at a workshop on Marine Sciences in East Africa. 14-16 November, 1989. Institute of Marine Sciences, University of Dar es Salaam.

Turner, E. 1977. Intertidal vegetation and commercial yields of Penaeid shrimp. *Transactions of the American Fisheries Society* 106(5):411-416.

Marine wetland interactions and policy in Tanzania

J.C. Horrill

Institute of Marine Sciences
P.O. Box 668
Zanzibar

Summary

The marine wetland habitat types of Tanzania are defined. The interactions between the ecosystems supporting these habitats are briefly described. The connections between these habitats demand a multi-sectoral approach to their management and the concept of integrated management, and its application to the marine wetlands of Mafia Island, is presented. Guidelines for the legislation and administration of such areas are also presented. The problems of implementation of such a policy in Tanzania and the suitability of this concept to the management of terrestrial wetlands is discussed.

Introduction

The Ramsar Convention defines marine wetlands as those areas from the highest extent of the tide to six metres below lowest tide level. This definition of marine wetlands includes a significant proportion of Tanzania's 900 km long, narrow coastal zone. The coastal zone supports a number of economically and socially important natural resources as well as possessing areas of international, regional and national significance with regard to conservation. Habitat types include: exposed hard coral, soft coral and algae dominated reefs, sheltered back reef systems, intertidal flats with hard and soft substrate, mangrove forests and extensive seagrass, algal, sponge and soft coral subtidal beds. These habitats support a high diversity of marine life, including a number of rare or endangered species such as turtles and dugong, as well as providing important feeding areas to migratory and resident birds. Although each of these habitat types superficially contains distinct communities, there are significant interactions between the ecosystem processes of individual habitats.

The close proximity of many reefs to the coast make them extremely prone to terrestrial influences of both natural and human origin. Coastal waters in Tanzania

125

have been traditionally exploited for fish, lobsters, octopus and shellfish (both for local consumption and for the curio trade) as well as live corals, coral rock, and mangrove poles for building purposes.

Many of the traditional practices result in degradation of reef flats and crests through trampling. Coral mining and pole cutting are particularly harmful as they can result in considerable habitat destruction. The greatest threat at present to the coastal environment, causing destruction of habitat on a large scale, is the illegal use of dynamite to stun and kill fish. This practice has increased since the late 1960s and has resulted in the destruction of many of Tanzania's coral reefs, including those around Dar es Salaam and Tanga. In addition, the disposal of sewage and chemical pollutants into coastal waters, especially around centres of rapid population and industrial growth, as well as mariculture, are increasing problems which will further degrade the marine environment if not carefully planned and managed.

Marine wetland interactions

The ecosystems of greatest importance, with regard to the increased productivity of coastal compared to oceanic waters, are those that support the mangrove forests, seagrass/algae beds and coral reefs. The health and productivity of these individual ecosystems is dependent upon a number of complex interactions. These interactions can be classified into five major types; physical factors, nutrients and dissolved organic matter, particulate organic matter, animal migration and human impact. Because of the interdependence of differing ecosystems, the deleterious effects of degradation of one particular ecosystem are not necessarily confined to that system. In addition, coastal ecosystems can be extremely vulnerable to terrestrial influences. This is especially pertinent to the marine wetlands of Tanzania which, because of the narrowness of the continental shelf, are often located in close proximity to the shoreline.

The possible effects of these interactions between marine ecosystems and terrestrial influences can be clearly illustrated by two examples from Tanzanian coastal waters; the use of explosives for fishing and the cutting of mangroves. The major effect of these activities has been habitat loss (Bryceson, 1981; Salm, 1983; Kudoja, 1985). The removal or destruction of natural breakwaters such as coral reefs has resulted in changes in current patterns and increased wave action causing loss of high value coastal land (e.g. Oyster Bay, Dar es Salaam). Problems of erosion have been exacerbated by the removal of mangroves which function as stabilisers of coastal sediments. Cutting of mangroves around freshwater outlets also lowers the effectiveness of natural systems to combat increased siltation caused by continued inland deforestation. Increased erosive capability, coupled with the loss of natural stabilisers, can lead to increased sediment loads in coastal waters. High levels of sediments are detrimental in that seagrass beds and coral reefs can be stifled, resulting in further degradation of these habitats.

Perhaps the largest physical influence of terrestrial origin is the freshwater, silt and nutrient input of the Rufiji River. The flow characteristics of this river may have been changed by the construction of dams at Mtera and Kidatu. Although great economic benefits accrue from these impoundments, they are not without negativeconsequences. It has been observed that parts of the Rufiji Delta is receding; the rate at Simba Uranga, calculated from aerial photographs taken in 1966 and 1989, has been estimated to be approximately 40 m/year (Pethick and Spencer, 1990). The eroding force of coastal wave action and currents is presently exceeding the deposition of silt in the delta, leading to beach erosion. One possible reason for this reduced sedimentation is that silt transported by the Rufiji River is being trapped behind these dams. The cutting of mangroves in the delta has probably exacerbated the problem.

The construction of dams also reduces the volume of freshwater and the associated flow of nutrients of terrestrial origin into the marine system. This often results in increased salinity and reduced productivity in estuarine and adjacent marine areas. The productivity of the Mafia Channel and associated fisheries (prawns and fish) are highly dependent on the Rufiji for the supply of nutrients.

Given the current dependence of the coastal population on marine related resources and that fisheries and tourism are important components of the Tanzanian economic recovery programme, the further degradation of the coastal environment could have disastrous social and economic consequences.

Current management policy

The current management strategy for marine wetlands has been a direct result of sectoral policies adopted by a wide range of agencies at national, regional and local level (Table 1).

Under the Fisheries Act, 1970, the Department of Fisheries is responsible for the management of all marine waters (including wetlands) from the mean high water mark to the limit of territorial waters. All land inland from the mean high water mark is administered by the National Planning Commission and the Ministry of Lands, Housing and Urban Development. Jurisdiction for mangroves, however, is administered through the Department of Forestry, even though mangrove stands exist above and below the high water mark. The Forest Ordinance of 1957 stipulates that all mangrove forests are Forestry Reserves. In addition, the Ministry of Trade and Industry has the mandate to issue licences to develop terrestrial land within coastal areas. This has resulted in licences being granted to utilise mangrove areas for salt production, even though these areas are protected through Forestry legislation. These issues are further complicated through developments initiated at Regional and District level, such as land acquisition for hotel developments. There has been little or no coordination of these often conflicting activities and no assessment of potential environmental impacts. The situation has been exacerbated by the current intense commercial interest in developing Tanzania's natural resources. Clearly, the sectoral approach adopted by these agencies has led to a confused and uncoordinated approach to the management of marine wetlands.

Table 1   Agencies involved in marine wetland management

1. National level	a)	Ministry of Tourism, Natural Resources and Environment
		(i) Division of Fisheries
		(ii) Division of Tourism
		(iii) Division of the Environment
		(iv) Division of Forestry and Bee Keeping
	b)	Ministry of Trade and Industry
	c)	Ministry of Lands, Housing and Urban Development
	d)	National Planning Commission
	e)	Ministry of Energy, Water and Mineral Resources
	f)	National Environmental Management Council
2. Regional level	a)	Regional Development Office
	b)	Natural Resources Office
	c)	Land Office
	d)	Health Office
	e)	Trade and Industry Inspectorate
	f)	Energy, Water and Mineral Resources Office
3. Local level	a)	District Development Office
	b)	District Natural Resources Office
		(i) Fisheries
		(ii) Forestry
	c)	District Land Office
	d)	District Council
	e)	District Administrative Office
	f)	Village Councils

The integrated management concept

The ultimate aim and reason for the adoption of an integrated management policy for marine wetlands is the achievement of various environmental, economic and social goals. The integrated management concept has evolved through the recognition of the interdependence of the ecosystems supporting the marine wetland habitats, and the failure of the traditional sectoral approach to coastal management to cope with increased pressure on marine resources.

The integrated management concept differs from the current policy in that a number of activities are permitted within the boundaries of large well defined areas, as long as they are compatible with the overall management objectives for that area. To ensure that benefits are available to all levels of the community, the management objectives for a particular area must be defined within a framework of local, national, regional, environmental, social and economic goals.

Because of the rigidity of former management strategies, there is a potential conflict between the conservation of the coastal environment and the development of economic

activities. This has often resulted in a reduction of living standards for local inhabitants, causing resentment and opposition to the establishment of other reserve areas. Options available in the planning of integrated management areas can minimise potential conflicts, if they are recognised when management objectives are defined for a particular area. Examples of integrated management areas are given in Table 2. From this table, it can be seen that there is a variety of internationally recognised areas that can be created to meet likely management objectives. The types of area that can be created range from development orientated Resource Reserves and Coastal Management Zones to more protective areas such as Biosphere Reserves and National Parks. Although these types of management area differ, to some extent, with regard to their stated main objectives, protection of the environment in which the resources occur is inherent in the main objective.

Achievement of primary objectives, within each of these areas, can be facilitated with minimal conflict of interest at the local level by the creation of a number of zones or user areas. Zoning within a particular integrated management area provides a second level of flexibility in management. Each zone can have differing levels or types of usage and should reflect the current or projected primary objectives for the particular area. These zones can range from areas of total human exclusion or restricted access, through a graduated regime, to areas which permit the controlled use or harvest of resources. Areas containing zones where access is restricted, for whatever reason, are known as core areas, with the area(s) between the core area(s) and the outer boundaries forming a buffer area. The buffer area contains those zones where controlled use or harvest of reef resources is permitted (Alcala and White, 1984; Kenchington, 1990). It is important to note that if the management objectives of a number of zones are compatible, several zones can be superimposed.

Table 2   A variety of integrated management areas, giving possible priority ranking to major objectives (taken and adapted from Polunin, 1990, and Salm and Clark, 1984)

Primary objectives	Area type							
	A	B	C	D	E	F	G	H
Protect ecosystem processes	1	2	2	2	1	2	1	2
Maintain biotic diversity	1	1	2	1	2	3	2	2
Research/environment monitoring	1	2	3	1	3	3	2	3
Education, protect aesthetic and/or cultural sites	3	2	1	2	3	3	2	3
Encourage rational development	3	3	3	3	2	1	1	1
Stabilise and maintain yield	1	2	3	2	1	1	2	2
Stimulate recreation/tourism	3	1	2	3	3	3	3	2

Priority ranking

1   Primary objective for management of area and resources
2   Not necessarily primary objective, but included as important
3   Included as an objective where applicable and whenever resources and other management objectives permit

Area type

A   Biosphere Reserve
B   National Park
C   Natural/Cultural Monument
D   Nature Reserve

E   Resource Reserve
F   Sustained yield harvest zone
G   Water quality control zone
H   Coastal management zone

Note: A more complete discussion is given by Salm and Clark (1984)

Regulation of activities to control the level or type of use within a zone can be achieved by the establishment of a permit system. An example of such a permit system in the Maldives is given in Table 3. The integrated management concept can therefore offer a great variety of management options to cope with the specific requirements of a given coastal system.

Development of an integrated management area

In general, the issues to be addressed in the management of such areas should be a matter of national policy. This ensures that the management objectives for the area will tackle the major problems of the coastal environment, with the support of the highest decision making bodies. Ideally, the creation of these areas should be part of a national or regional strategy to facilitate specified interaction with already established legislation and agencies such as the Planning Commission and the Department of Fisheries. Once the management objectives for the coastal environment have been established, a zonation policy can address practical means by which those objectives can be achieved.

The planning process for an integrated management area would entail development of a legislative base, the establishment of an administrative authority, the definition of management objectives, and the formulation of a detailed plan to achieve management objectives.

The initiation of an integrated management policy is clearly a complex process and can require significant revision of existing policies. Such a policy has been adopted for the integrated management of marine wetlands in Tanzania by the inception of a multi-user marine management area at Mafia Island. If successful, this policy could then be extended to encompass further areas of the Tanzanian coastline. The following sections describe the approach that has been taken in the attempt to establish the Mafia Island multi-user management area.

Development of a legislative base

Development of a legislative base can be complex. Through the traditional sectoral management policy, a large amount of often conflicting legislation can exist. The basic problem is that effective management of the coastal areas must be supported by legislation that is not delineated at the land-sea interface. This is because certain land based activities, such as industrial and domestic pollution, often affect the marine environment. Legislation must be either drafted or created by the modification of existing legislation so that areas of responsibility between authorities are defined unambiguously.

In general, the legislation should ensure that there is enough detail for:

1. Correct implementation and compliance.
2. Clear delineation of boundaries.

Table 3   A conceptual permit system for activity regulation within different zone types in the Maldives (Source: Kenchington, 1990)

Activity	Zone type					
	1	2	3	4	5	6
Reclamation	P	P	P	X	X	X
Building	P	P	P	P	P1	X
Sewage	P	P	P	P	P1	X
Industrial development	P	X	X	X	X	X
Commercial development	P	P	X	X	X	X
Coral mining	P	P	P	X	X	X
Tourism development	P	P	P	X	X	X
Tourist activities	P	P	P	P	X	X
Mariculture	P	P	P	X	P1	X
Subsistence fishery	/	/	/	X	X	X
Commercial fishery	/	/	X	X	X	X
Shell/coral collection	/	/	/	X	X	X
Net fishing	P	P	P	X	X	X
Boating	P	P	/	/	X	X
Dive/snorkel	/	/	/	/	X	X
Scientific research	/	/	/	/	P	P2

Zone type

1   Development general use zone
2   General use commercial zone
3   General use subsistence zone
4   National Park zone
5   Scientific research zone
6   Nature Reserve

Activity

/   Allowed as right
P   Allowed subject to permit
P1   Permitted only in connection with approved research
P2   Permitted only for non-manipulative research that cannot be conducted elsewhere
X   Not allowed

3. Provision of adequate statements of authority and precedence.
4. Provision of adequate infrastructure and support to ensure the undertaking of the required tasks.

The overall goal(s) to be achieved by the creation of an integrated management area, and the objectives of that area in the pursuance of that goal(s), should also be included in legislation. If zones with their own set of objectives are to be created, then legislation should state the types of zones, their objectives and provide adequate detail to control activities and protect resources. These latter provisions should ideally override all conflicting legislation within the constraints of international law. Jurisdiction of various agencies, responsibility, account-ability and capacity should be stated to ensure the management objectives and basic goals are achieved. Provisions for the implementation of various manage-ment techniques (e.g. temporary closure to allow resource recovery) should also be included.

Creation of a strong legislative base is imperative to the success of integrated management areas. Formulation of the legislation is a complex process involving the review of all existing or proposed legislation that could affect the coastal zone. Once a firm commitment to develop such an integrated coastal policy has been made, drafting and enactment of the legislation should be the first priority.

The establishment of an administrative authority

The integrated coastal management administrative authority should be defined in the legislation. Ideally the authority should grow from existing agencies, unless this is impractical or there is overwhelming public and political support for the creation of a new organisation. The current administration of marine wetlands (see earlier) is extremely complicated and has resulted in the adoption of policies with conflicting goals. This has led to the proposition that a new authority be created to administer the integrated management of the Mafia Island multi-user marine area. Provision will have to be made for the interaction of the authority with other central and local governmental agencies as well as non-governmental organisa-tions, scientific research institutions and user groups (especially local users). This may be possible by the creation of advisory and local village committees which would inform, advise and interact with the authority's activities.

Definition of goals and objectives

The definition of management goals, and hence objectives, is the first and most important step in the development of an integrated policy. The overall goals for marine wetland resource management are likely to include the achievement of maximum sustainable economic benefit from long term yield of natural resources, maintenance of the condition and productivity of the natural environment, and the allocation of resources between competing uses and users. The establishment of protected areas for tourism and conservation is also to be considered. It follows that the likely goals for the integrated management of Mafia Island could be:

1. To protect pristine ecosystem processes and areas of high species and genetic diversity.
2. To stimulate the rational development of unexploited natural resources including tourism.
3. To promote sustainability of existing resource use, incorporating recovery strategies for overexploited resources.

The way these goals are achieved depends on the socio-economic structure and government decision making processes of the country. It is important in defining the objectives that a balanced outlook between protection of the environment and the development of resources is maintained. A bias towards protection may deprive local inhabitants of their livelihood and therefore result in their non-cooperation. The consequence of this will inevitably be the failure of the management area. Conversely, bias toward development may result in overexploitation and degradation of nationally and internationally important resources. To achieve the management goals, management objectives have to be defined in the context of the past, present and likely future uses for the area. For marine wetland areas, management objectives would need to take the following activities into account:

- preservation of undisturbed natural environments;
- protection of breeding areas of endangered species;
- protection of breeding areas of commercially important species;
- scientific research;
- environmental education including public awareness;
- non-extractive recreation and tourism;
- regulated extractive recreation and tourism;
- subsistence fishing (including non-conventional species);
- commercial fishing (including non-conventional species);
- mariculture (farming of marine algae, prawns, fish);
- shipping, including dredging of navigational channels, construction of navigational aids, harbours, breakwaters and jetties;
- extraction of construction materials;
- construction of tourist facilities including marinas;
- residential construction;
- light industry;
- hydrocarbon drilling;
- disposal of domestic, commercial and industrial wastes;
- heavy industry;
- coastal and seabed mining.

Formulation of a plan for management

Central to the success of any multi-user area is the formulation of a practical plan for the management of that area. Development of such a plan is a complex process requiring accurate information on the area under consideration and the consultation of resource users at all levels.

Pre-plan information

To gain the information to develop such a plan, it is necessary to initiate a study to achieve a reasonable understanding of the nature, condition, and resources of the area and its past, present, likely and possible future uses. The study should, therefore, examine considerations of the physical, biological and socio-economic environments and problems associated with rational development.

Identification of zone type and site selection

It is then possible to identify the type of zones to be included within a given area. The following sub-sections give an example of how this may be achieved.

Identification of zone type

The second stage of development of a multi-user area, and the method by which the management concept approaches the problem of avoidance or reduction of potential conflicts of interest between differing user groups, is the creation of a number of zones or user areas. Each zone has a defined management objective or set of management objectives. The activities allowed within that zone would be those compatible with the objective(s), other activities would not be permitted or would be subject to regulation.

Considering the likely overall goals for the Mafia area, the physical and biological characteristics, current resource use (Horrill, 1991; Horrill and Ngoile, 1991) and the activities that could take place, then the type of zones that could be created are:

1. General Use Zone
2. Specified Use Zone
3. Protected Zone.

The General Use and Specified Use Zones would act as buffer areas for the Protected Zone(s) which would constitute the core area(s).

Site selection

Although the zoning plan will not be finalised until after considerable consultation and discussion with user groups and concerned agencies, a useful starting point for the formulation of the boundaries of any zones is to examine what an ardent exponent of one of the overall goals would propose. The goals discussed previously were to protect pristine ecosystem processes and areas of high species and genetic diversity; to stimulate the rational development of unexploited natural resources including tourism; to promote sustainability of existing resource use incorporating recovery strategies for overexploited resources. The developer would want the existing areas of use to be fully exploited and to develop those areas which are not exploited at present. This essentially entails the opening of all areas to commercial development. The supporter of tourist development would advocate that all areas of high aesthetic value be made available for tourist use activities such as snorkeling, diving and sports fishing should be retained exclusively for these interests. The preservationist would want to protect all areas from development and tourism.

Superimposition of areas of interest to user groups identifies those zones of potential conflict of interest. In many cases, the areas deemed suitable for tourism are those best conserved. With the developer also wanting to utilise these areas, there is a possible three way conflict of interest. This then gives a starting point for discussions involving all interested parties and/or agencies. The final partitioning of these areas will eventually depend on the results of these discussions and consultations, and the priority given to particular management objectives.

Discussion

Although integrated management strategies are being increasingly employed in many countries to conserve and protect natural resources and pristine habitats, the major obstacle to their adoption is that the formulation of such a strategy can be difficult and complicated. It must be stated, however, that many of these difficulties, if ignored or avoided during the planning stages, can lead to severe and insurmountable problems in the implementation of any integrated management project. The rationale to the strategy described in this document, therefore, is to identify and overcome all likely problems before any management plan is implemented.

It is extremely important to involve the local users in all stages of the formulation of an integrated management policy. This may often include education on the type of management under consideration, so as to maximise the input of relevant information from the local community. Accurate and realistic assessments of local needs and aspirations are crucial to the success of integrated management. As integrated management is often an evolving process, local users must also be able to participate in future decision making processes once an area has been established. Adherence to a community orientated policy, coupled with an extensive education programme, should ensure minimum conflict between management and local communities.

The potential difficulties in pursuing such a strategy for marine wetlands in mainland Tanzania, led to the adoption of Mafia Island as a pilot study. The boundaries of the integrated management area at Mafia are within one administrative district to facilitate planning and implementation. If the management of this area proves successful, then the outlined strategy would greatly facilitate the extension of integrated management of marine wetlands to other areas. A significant extension would be to the marine wetlands and coastal area associated with the Rufiji Delta and then many of the marine processes occurring in Tanzanian coastal waters would be under some kind of practical management regime.

It is recommended that if this strategy for the management of marine wetlands is adopted, a similar approach be taken for the management of terrestrial wetlands. Given current thinking on the protection of ecosystem processes, the large effect of river associated, terrestrial wetlands on marine systems and the future management plans for marine wetlands, it is recommended that a significant portion of the Rufiji River system be considered as a pilot study area for the management of terrestrial wetlands. Although this may seem a large undertaking, the social, economic and environmental benefits of having the inter-connected ecosystem processes of the Rufiji River system and associated marine wetlands under sustainable management would be enormous.

Bibliography

Alcala, A.C. and A.T. White. 1984. Options for management. Pages 31-40. In: R.A. Kenchington and B.E.T. Hudson (Eds). *Coral Reef Management Handbook*. UNESCO, Indonesia.

Bryceson, I. 1981. A review of some problems of tropical marine conservation with particular reference to the Tanzanian coast. *Biol. Conserv.* 20:163-171.

Horrill, J.C. 1991. Mafia Island Project. Report No. 1, July 1990 to March 1991. Frontier-Tanzania. The Society for Environmental Exploration, London, U.K. 24 pp.

Horrill, J.C. and M.A.K. Ngoile. 1991. Mafia Island Project. Report No. 2, September 1991. Results of the physical, biological and resource use surveys: Rationale for the development of a management strategy. Frontier-Tanzania. The Society for Environmental Exploration, London, U.K. 46 pp.

Kenchington, R.A. 1990. *Managing Marine Environments*. Taylor and Francis, New York Inc. 221 pp.

Kudoja, W.M. 1985. The Tanzanian coral reefs at risk. *Proc. 5th Int. Coral Reef Cong., Tahiti* 2:209.

Pethick, J. and T. Spencer. 1990. Mangrove response to sea level rise: The Rufiji Delta, Tanzania. The Society for Environmental Exploration, London, U.K. 6 pp.

Polunin, N.V.C. 1990. Marine Regulated Areas: An Expanded Approach for the Tropics. *Resource Management and Optimization* 7:283-299.

Salm, R.V. 1983. Coral reefs of the West Indian Ocean: a threatened heritage. *Ambio* 12:349-353.

Salm, R.V. and J.R. Clark. 1984. *Marine and coastal protected areas: A guide for planners and managers*, 2nd edn, IUCN, Geneva. 302 pp.

Policy development for wetland management

P. Mafabi

National Wetlands Conservation and Management Programme
P.O. Box 9629
Kampala
Uganda

Summary

The Wetlands Programme within the Ministry of Water, Energy, Minerals and Environment Protection is described as well as its major activity of developing a national policy on wetlands, by advising the various branches of government and consulting with people who live in and use wetlands. The programme also provides technical information for the planning of wetland activities and oversees developments in wetlands.

Introduction

About 10% of Uganda's total land area, 205,000 km^2, is occupied by wetlands and historically these areas were referred to as wastelands. The belief that wetlands, especially marshes, are a major source of diseases like malaria and bilharzia has discouraged their utilisation. Lind (1956) notes that although they occupy a large area of Uganda, these waterlogged areas have hitherto attracted little attention, being considered useless except to provide a few fish and building materials in a country where good agricultural land was plentiful. This notion has apparently changed and over the last 20 years the wetland resource has been put under considerable pressure from agriculture resulting in the draining of many wetlands and modification of several others.

However, there is growing concern within the government that much of the agriculture on wetland soils is not sustainable and, therefore, there is need to develop a policy that will ensure sustainable and national utilisation of wetland resources.

This paper examines some of the steps taken to prepare a national wetlands policy for Uganda.

The need for a national wetlands policy

Uganda's economy is based almost entirely on agriculture, and the increasing population places a heavy strain on traditional, cultivable land. This has led to encroachment into forest resources, game reserves and the reclamation of swamps. The varied and diverse wetland resources are found at altitudes ranging from 1,134 m, on the shores of Lake Victoria, to over 4,000 m on the Rwenzori Mountains. Although they occupy a large area of the country, these waterlogged areas have attracted little attention and were considered useless except to provide some fish (lung fish, *Protopterus* spp.; catfish, *Clarias* spp.), building materials and raw materials for handcrafts. For a long time there was plenty of agricultural land elsewhere, although wetland edges were used to produce millet, sweet potatoes and other food crops.

Peoples' perception of wetland values have varied with time and other factors. They have ranged from an attitude where people viewed wetlands as wastelands to the present trend where some people view wetlands as opportunities for development.

A survey of people in some of the wetland areas found mixed feelings about wetlands. In one area, some people felt that wetlands should be used for cattle grazing to produce milk while others felt that wetlands were communal areas which should not be monopolised by a few individuals. In another area, some felt that wetlands were not very useful except for the provision of materials for thatching and making crafts. Such people preferred to drain wetlands to grow crops such as pineapples and bananas. Other people in the same area clearly stated that wetlands played a vital role in groundwater regulation. People near Kampala thought that all wetlands should be conserved and gazetted so that they could be protected by law. In Doho, in eastern Uganda, the people had been severely affected by floods; so to them the creation of a rice scheme and the controlling of floods was a relief. Most people viewed wetlands as wastelands which could be put to better use.

It was clear from this survey that there was a variety of opinions about wetlands and that people perceived wetland values differently. In such circumstances, a policy is needed that will guide the proper management and rational utilisation of wetlands, while taking cognisance of the needs and aspirations of people living around the resource.

One of the main objectives of the National Wetlands Programme is to develop a wetlands policy that will provide a coherent framework for rational management of wetlands. The lack of accurate information on the distribution and status of many of Uganda's wetlands gives rise to the need for a thorough inventory and the production of a specialised wetland map.

Stages in policy development

Some districts have by-laws restricting agricultural use of wetlands but, at present, the only other legal protection for most wetlands is as follows:

1. That they are state land and may not be owned by private individuals.
2. A September 1986 circular, from the Ministry of Environment Protection to all District Administrators, suspending all large scale drainage activities pending development of a national policy.

The inter-ministerial approach

Since wetlands cover a broad range of land and water types, they are affected by almost all aspects of government policy expressed by sectoral ministries. Uganda happens to be in a situation where inter-sectoral inconsistencies are pronounced. The wetlands programme recognised this and so a first step in developing a policy was to involve ministries and departments whose activities were relevant to, or had a direct bearing on, wetlands.

An inter-ministerial committee, chaired by the Permanent Secretary in the Ministry of Environment Protection, was set up in August 1989 and had its first meeting in November 1989.

In addition to the Environment Ministry[1], the committee comprises the following ministries and departments: Agriculture, Animal Industry and Fisheries, Water and Mineral Development, Land and Survey, Planning and Economic Development, Energy, Health, Local Government, and Justice. The following government departments or institutions are also represented: Uganda Freshwater Fisheries Research Organisation, Makerere University Institute of Environment and Natural Resources, Uganda National Parks, Game Department, and Department of Meteorology.

The most important feature of the Inter-Ministerial Committee is that it establishes an approved channel of communication, and the Project Management Unit may take advantage of this in soliciting action and support from the various ministries and departments.

Phase 1 activities of the Wetlands Programme resulted in the preparation of a draft policy. This process was facilitated by the implementation of the Inter-Ministerial Committee. In addition to proposals and suggestions made in the Committee meetings, the policy has incorporated a section on *Guidelines for Developers*, which intends to provide specific technical guidance to users of wetlands.

---

1 The Ministry of Environment Protection changed to the Ministry of Water, Energy and Environment Protection (MWEMEP) in 1991.

District Development Committees

Once formulated, the policy will have to be implemented at the grassroots level and be integrated into the overall development of local communities. This is in accordance with the new government policy of decentralising development by strengthening the District Development Committees (DDCs). It is in recognition of this fact that DDCs were consulted and involved in discussions of the draft policy. Districts were selected on the basis of the pressures that have been inflicted upon their wetlands. Consultation involved project personnel presenting the draft policy to full meetings of the DDCs and briefing members on its contents. It is anticipated that feedback from the DDCs will amend the draft in a positive way that will make it a workable policy.

Review of past legislation

Although there is no policy or law regarding wetlands *per se,* there are many sections within the existing legislation that have some relevance to wetland issues and these are currently being reviewed. The review is expected to result in suggestions for the codification of the draft policy into appropriate legislation, through consultation with members of the Inter-Ministerial Committee and the DDCs.

Cardinal points in the policy

The most important product of the Wetlands Programme will be a management policy and legislative package to assist the Environment Ministry (MWEMEP) in its role of ensuring that wetlands are managed on a sustainable basis. The six cardinal points of the proposed policy and guidelines for management are given below.

Policy on drainage activities

Under no circumstances may a wetland be drained. Users of a wetland must ensure that the overall balance is maintained, however, ridging and trenching may be performed within a wetland allowing growth of crops requiring drier soils, as long as the water level does not fall below the established water table. When carrying out bunding or trenching, the head waters may not be modified.

Policy on land tenure

The Land Commission should seek clearance from the MWEMEP before allocating any wetland area.

The people living around a wetland may have derived benefits from that wetland for many years, such as cutting of reeds, water supply, fishing and grazing. Any change in usage of a wetland must allow those uses to continue without exclusion of the people.

In cases where there is clear evidence of environmental damage caused to a wetland, MWEMEP will recommend that the outstanding lease be revoked. Arbitration in such cases will be determined by an Environment Impact Assessment (EIA), coordinated and assessed by MWEMEP with inter-ministerial collaboration.

Policy on water supply and effluent treatment

Wetlands, serving as water supplies or receiving effluent as part of a designed service to an urban centre, should be fully protected from any encroachment, drainage or modification. Where there is clear evidence of damage to a wetland receiving effluent, MWEMEP will require the local and urban authorities to reconstruct such a wetland and improve treatment of effluent.

Policy on recovery of previously drained wetlands

Action may be taken to regenerate or restore a wetland that has suffered non-sustainable use. This action will be governed by appropriate EIA and Inter-Ministerial Review chaired by MWEMEP.

Policy on Environment Impact Assessment

All proposed modifications, restorations, drainage or impacts upon wetlands should be subject to an EIA approved by MWEMEP. However, exceptions will be granted to closely defined, subsistence farming activities.

Policy on biological conservation of wetlands

In consultation with the Ministry of Tourism, Wildlife, and Antiquities, MWEMEP proposes to establish full protection for certain wetlands of important biological diversity. No proposal for modification, drainage or other impacts will be entertained for wetlands so protected. The Lake George wetlands have been accorded the status of 'wetlands of international importance' under the Ramsar Convention. Plans are in hand to protect the unique swamp forests at Sango Bay on the shores of Lake Victoria.

Long term implementation of the policy

In the long term, the conservation and management of wetlands will be effective only if rural communities appreciate the values of wetlands and have a stake in the utilisation of these resources.

In this way, the local people will have the incentive to protect and conserve wetlands. Both the Wetlands Programme and MWEMEP must strive through the DDCs to instill the necessary local decision making structures for wetland management.

Bibliography

Lind, E.M. 1956. Studies in Uganda swamps. *Uganda Journal* 20:166-176.

The Zambian Wetlands Project: a Zambian experience

P.M. Chooye

Community Development Coordinator
WWF-Zambia Wetlands Project
Post Bag 1
Chilanga
Zambia

Summary

The Zambian Wetlands Programme is organised around conservation and sustainable utilisation of wetland products at two major wetland sites in the country. The programme mobilises local people to carry out the planning and control of its projects and ensures that government, through the National Parks and Wildlife Service, provides technical assistance to the programme and helps to support the conservation efforts of local authorities and people.

Introduction

Zambia is a landlocked country in southern Africa, located between 8 and 19°S, and 22 and 34°E, is bordered by Zaire, Tanzania, Malawi, Mozambique, Zimbabwe, Namibia, Angola and Botswana, and has a land area of 753,972 km². The land surface is predominantly an elevated plateau, dominated by *Miombo* woodland, which covers about 70% of the country.

Zambia is drained by the Zambezi and Luapula River systems. The former drains into the Indian Ocean while the latter is part of the Congo system which drains into the Atlantic Ocean. At least 6% of Zambia's area may be classified as wetlands.

Project core areas

The WWF-Zambia Wetlands Project is confined to two major wetland areas which are important refuges for wildlife, including Kafue lechwe (*Kobus leche kafuenis*), black lechwe (*Kobus leche smithemani*), Burchell's zebra (*Equus burchelli*), si-tatunga (*Tragelaphus spekei*), tsessebe (*Damaliscus lunatus*), wattled crane (*Bugeranus carunculatus*) and shoebill (*Balaeniceps rex*).

Bangweulu Basin

The Bangweulu Basin is roughly circular with an area of approximately 31,000 km². It is famous for its fisheries and wildlife resources and includes parts of three National Parks and six Game Management Areas. The basin is dissected by numerous rivers, of which 17 flow into the Bangweulu Swamp. Numerous lakes, swamps, floodplains and flats comprise the 11,900 km² wetland which is the largest and most diversified in Zambia. In 1969, a population of 940,000 persons was supported on the islands and the fringes of the wetlands.

Kafue Flats

The entire Kafue Basin is 154,000 km² in area while the Kafue Flats are approximately 6,500 km² of floodplain and grassland. Two National Parks and a Game Management Area are found within the Kafue Flats. The area is significant for its wildlife (principal species are Kafue Lechwe and zebra), fisheries and livestock grazing.

Two dams (Kafue Gorge and Itezhi-tezhi) were constructed on the Kafue River for the Kafue Hydroelectric Scheme and their influence has made the Kafue Flats the most disturbed wetlands in Zambia.

Community participation in natural resources conservation

Conservation of nature and the environment in Zambia is largely the responsibility of the government through the Ministry of Tourism, Lands and Environment. More recently, non-governmental organisations have become increasingly involved in conservation. The WWF-Zambia Wetlands Project, initiated in August 1986 as a special project under the National Parks and Wildlife Service (NPWS), has established a community based project for the conservation and management of wetlands. The project is concerned with the conservation of nature and the environment, in general, and the conservation of wildlife in particular. The project is active in the Bangweulu Swamps and the Kafue Flats. Both areas are ecologically and economically significant as they are important for fisheries, wildlife and, in the Kafue Flats, grazing.

Today, it is unusual to suggest a conservation strategy which is not participatory. Community involvement seems desirable and should be required by conservation agencies as no conservation strategy can succeed without the people's support. Biological resources, such as forests, fish, wildlife and wetlands, are being exploited at unsustainable rates. Both conservation and development agencies are therefore busy searching for approaches to resource management which will ensure sustainable use without degrading the resource base. The 'top-down', government-managed conservation projects are not only ineffective but also prohibitively expensive; they are tightly controlled, centrally managed and are dominated by technical experts.

If rural people could be encouraged to participate in the decisions regarding the use of communal resources, for example grazing land or forests, then they would be more likely to actively protect these resources. In seeking to promote this understanding and to bring about greater participation, Tola (1986) suggested that the following four basic principles could help to advance community participation within conservation projects.

1. Rural people are more prepared to participate when they feel the need for conservation.

2. Rural people make rational decisions in the context of their own environment and circumstances rather than those prescribed by the government or project staff.

3. Voluntary local commitment of labour, time, material and money to a conservation project is a necessary condition for breaking patterns of conservation paternalism which reinforces local passivity and indifference.

4. Local control of the amount, quality and (especially) the distribution of benefits from conservation activities is directly related to those activities becoming self sustaining.

Implementation and institutional arrangements

The Zambia Wetlands Project was developed and is implemented within the framework of existing institutions. The target communities are the indigenous residents of 14 chiefdoms of the Kafue Flats and Bangweulu Swamps. To some extent, target communities also include non-indigenous (immigrant) populations and public servants of the various agencies concerned with the management, regulation and control of project areas.

The indigenous people of the Kafue Flats, the Illa and Tonga, are traditionally cattle keeping people who also engage in subsistence and small scale commercial agriculture mainly on the periphery of the wetlands. In the Bangweulu Swamps, the Bisa, Ushi and Unga are traditionally hunters and fishermen.

Extensive and exhaustive consultations were carried out with the traditional chiefs and political and government officials; public meetings were held with the local people to win their confidence and to engender support for the project. These initiatives resulted in the formation of Community Development Units (CDUs), at the grassroots level, and Wetland Management Authorities (WMAs). In both the Kafue Flats and Bangweulu Swamps, four WMAs have been established, drawing membership from 13 of the 14 chiefdoms. The members of both the CDUs and the

WMAs were elected by the community. The seventh chiefdom in the Kafue Flats did not participate in the project because of suspicion resulting from past loss of grazing land to the Nakambala Sugar Estate, a national irrigation scheme.

The chairmen of the CDUs are elected and, in some cases, the chiefs are the chairmen. In the previous One Party State of government, the chairmen of the WMAs were the District Governors of the principal areas. In the current Multi-Party Democratic System, it is anticipated that the District Executive Secretaries will assume the chairmanships of WMAs. Elected members from the CDUs constitute membership of the WMAs.

The Authorities make their own decisions regarding priorities and the use of information, funds and resources available to them for their own development programmes. Within the framework of the existing legislation and Wetlands Management Plans, the WMAs may collaborate with district development officers, line department staff and staff of other organisations to reinforce and coordinate community development activities in the project areas. The chiefs select reliable young men to train as village scouts who live in the community. They report cases of poaching to NPWS scouts who are law enforcement officers. The members of the community voluntarily report cases of poaching involving both the local people and outsiders. Anti-poaching programmes are usually planned on the basis of information received.

Economic and social benefits for conserving natural resources

There is need to conserve natural resources for many reasons, including the fact that natural resources earn profits from tourism and wildlife utilisation and harvesting. It is necessary to ensure that a fair share of these profits are returned to the local people who are incurring the opportunity cost of not harvesting the resource. In Zambia, the local communities who share land with wildlife have already begun to receive benefits from their conservation efforts. The Wetlands Project has used the ADMADE (Administrative Management Design Programmes for Game Management Areas) programme (Lewis *et al.*, 1989) policy framework to establish a means of funding the activities of the WMAs from wildlife revenues. This facility allows the Authorities to retain 50% of statutory (government) revenues and all non-statutory revenues from certain categories of wildlife utilisation in ADMADE programme areas, including revenues from hunting, cropping and donations. These revenues accrue to the Wildlife Conservation Revolving Fund, which later apportions them to the WMAs for allocation to the CDUs according to the following formula:

- 40% to local wildlife management activities (to meet fuel costs, rations and salaries for village scouts);
- 35% to local community development activities;

- 15% to National Parks and Wildlife Service (to meet costs of programme administration);
- 10% to ADMADE for programme administration.

The WMAs have developed their own fund-generating ventures; for example a community shop, self-catering camps and grinding mills have been established. The revenue generated, in both local and foreign currency, is banked in the Development Accounts of the Authorities.

As a consequence of sharing benefits derived from conservation, progress in the conservation of wildlife has been significant. The estimated increase in the population of Kafue lechwe has been from 41,000 in 1983 to 45,000 in 1988 (Howard and Jeffery, 1983; Kampamba *et al.*, 1990). Assuming that environmental conditions are not currently limiting population growth, the population is expected to increase by approximately 10% *per annum*.

As the people are usually interested in local development, the Wetlands Project has financed rural development projects such as schools, clinics, water wells and dams with funds from 'Debt for Nature Swap' and direct WWF funding.

Constraints to conservation programmes

Erosion of traditional systems

There is often a lack of identification with common or public property, an attitude which sees national conservation schemes as alien or unwanted. In the past, hunting was strictly controlled by the chiefs. A traditional form of hunting called 'chila' (communal hunting) was practised by the local people of the Kafue Flats, in the months of May and August. Although the method used was unsophisticated, hunting was controlled, and severe, punitive measures were taken against poachers.

The trend towards centralised government, in both pre- and post-independence, resulted in the alienation of the traditional authorities from their hunting rights and thus their interest in the control of the wildlife resource. For example, when the colonial government created national parks and game management areas in Zambia, indigenous local people were not consulted and their traditional systems of conservation were eroded; the people were alienated and became eager exploiters, anxious to get the material benefits of the modern society. Until the Wetlands Project was established, local support for conservation had been very low and illegal hunting of wildlife, especially buffalo (*Syncerus caffer*), blue wildebeest (*Connochaetes taurinus*) and greater kudu (*Tragelaphus strepsiceros*), reached such high levels that extermination of these species was a reality in some areas. Despite strengthened law enforcement, villagers welcomed poachers for a share in the harvested meat.

When the project was being established in the Kafue Flats, the villagers admitted to assisting poachers because they felt that they no longer had the responsibility to protect the wildlife. The central government, with inadequate management capacity, had claimed responsibility over a resource it could not control and manage properly. Following the establishment of the project, the local communities' interests in the wildlife resource is gradually being restored and local people volunteer as vigilantes.

Poverty

Another constraint to community based nature conservation is poverty among the indigenous communities. In the last 27 years of Zambia's independence, there has been a deterioration of the standard of living in both the urban and rural areas. This has seriously threatened natural resources as communities attempt to earn a living through indiscriminate fishing and destruction of woodlands for fuel wood or charcoal. A community based, natural resource project should consider redressing the stubborn persistence of hunger, poverty and unemployment by encouraging small scale industries.

Education

Lack of information or community education can be a major constraint to community based conservation. Conservation of natural resources needs an approach in which the purpose of, and the benefits to be derived from, the project should be made clear to everyone. The Zambia Wetlands Project has established a community conservation training centre at Lochinvar, in order to inform, teach and educate the local communities and the general public of the need to protect and conserve the precious resources.

Other constraints

Local communities are sometimes suspicious of new projects because they have been neglected or badly treated in the past.

Lack of coordination among conservation agencies serving the same community can lead to confusion amongst the people, especially if the agencies have conflicting goals.

Attempts still continue to impose 'top-down' projects or development schemes which fail to address community needs.

Conclusion

There is an urgent need to find appropriate ways of conserving natural resources. Successful conservation is more likely when the local community knows the value of the resources. The foundation of any serious conservation strategy is the support of the local community and such support is gained through public awareness and the involvement of the beneficiaries. In many cases the destruction of the resources is not deliberate but due to ignorance.

A deliberate attempt should be made to ensure that local communities are made part of the conservation project's planning process from the earliest stages. The WWF-Zambia Wetlands Project has made it possible for local communities to benefit from the co-operative management of their traditional resources. As far as possible, revenues from biological resources should be returned to support local village economies.

Bibliography

Howard, G.W. and R.C.V. Jeffery. 1983. Kafue lechwe population status, 1981-1983. Report to the Director, NPWS, Chilanga. Mimeo.

Jeffery, R.C.V. 1992. The Kafue flats of Zambia - A case study. Pages 57-70. In: T. Matiza and H.N. Chabwela (Eds). *Wetlands Conservation Conference for Southern Africa. Proceedings of the Southern African Development Coordination Conference.* Gaberone, Botswana, 3-5 June, 1991. IUCN, Gland, Switzerland. x + 224 pp.

Jeffery, R.C.V., H.N. Chabwela, G. Howard and P.J. Dugan. 1992. *Managing the Wetlands of Kafue Flats and Bangweulu Basin. Proceedings of the WWF-Zambia Wetlands Project Workshop.* 5-7 November, 1986. Kafue National Park, Zambia. IUCN, Gland, Switzerland.

Kampamba, G., B. Kamweneshe, R. Nefdt and R.C.V. Jeffery. 1991. Large wildlife mammal surveys of the Kafue Flats. Report to the Director, NPWS, Chilanga. Mimeo.

Lewis, D.M., A.N. Mwenya and G.B. Kaweche. 1989. African solutions to wildlife problems in Africa. Insights from a community based project in Zambia. National Parks and Wildlife Service of Zambia, Chilanga. Unpublished report.

Oakley, P. 1989. *The concept of participation in development.* University of Reading, UK. pp. 9-11.

Tola, A. 1986. Who is concerned? *Splash* 2(1):10-12.

The Ramsar Convention:
its role in promoting wise use of African wetlands and the formation of the Kenya Wetlands Working Group

S.G. Njuguna

Centre for Biodiversity
National Museums of Kenya
P.O. Box 40658
Nairobi
Kenya

Introduction

The Convention on Wetlands of International Importance especially as Waterfowl Habitat is sometimes known as the Ramsar Convention because the text of the Convention was adopted in the Iranian city of Ramsar in 1971. It is the first of the five modern global conventions on conservation and wise use of natural resources; the others are World Heritage, CITES, Migratory Species and Biodiversity. The Ramsar Convention is the only convention which deals with a specific habitat, the wetlands. It is an inter-governmental treaty which provides the framework for the conservation of wetland habitats.

Wetlands are very important for their ecological processes as well as their rich biodiversity. It is the broad objective of the Convention to stem the loss of wetlands and to ensure their conservation. Governments which join the Ramsar Convention accept four principal obligations:

1. To designate at least one wetland in their territory for the List of Wetlands of International Importance and to maintain the ecological character of the designated wetlands.

2. To make 'wise use' of all wetlands in their territory, whether or not they are included in the above list. The Contracting Parties have adopted guidelines on wise use which call for the establishment of national wetland policies.

3. To consult with one another about implementation of the Convention, in particular with regard to shared wetland systems, shared species and development aid affecting wetlands.

4.   To establish nature reserves in wetlands, whether or not they are designated for the list. Special approaches are required for such reserve creation and management; wetland reserves are different from other reserves as they are more likely to be seriously affected by activities well outside their boundaries.

The Convention entered into force on 21 December 1975 and has currently a membership of nearly 70 governments including 17 from the African region (Table 1). These Contracting Parties have designated over 550 wetlands, covering more than 33 million hectares (i.e. an area nearly equivalent to the size of Zimbabwe) for the Ramsar List.

The Convention uses an extremely broad definition of wetlands, encompassing shallow coastal areas, estuaries, coral reefs and tundra, as well as rivers, lakes, marshes, and temporary and artificial water bodies (Ramsar Convention Bureau, 1992).

Table 1   Contracting Parties to the Ramsar Convention in Africa

Country	Date convention came into force	Number of wetlands designated	Areas of wetlands (ha)
South Africa	21.12.75	7	208,044
Senegal	11.11.77	4	99,720
Morocco	20.10.80	4	10,580
Tunisia	24.03.81	1	12,600
Mauritania	22.02.83	1	1,173,000
Algeria	04.03.84	2	4,900
Gabon	30.04.87	3	1,080,000
Niger	30.08.87	1	220,000
Mali	25.09.87	3	162,000
Ghana	22.06.88	1	7,260
Uganda	04.07.88	1	15,000
Egypt	09.09.88	2	105,000
Guinea-Bissau	09.05.90	1	39,098
Kenya	05.10.90	1	18,800
Chad	13.10.90	1	195,000
Burkina Faso	27.10.90	3	299,200
Zambia	28.12.91	2	333,000

Criteria for identifying wetlands of international importance

A wetland is suitable for inclusion in the Ramsar List of Wetlands of International Importance if it meets any one of the criteria set out below (RAMSAR, 1990a):

1. Criteria for assessing the value of representative or unique wetlands

A wetland is considered internationally important if it is a particularly good example of a specific type of wetland characteristic of its region.

2. General criteria for using plants or animals to identify wetlands of importance

A wetland should be considered internationally important if:

a) it supports an appreciable assemblage of rare, vulnerable or endangered species or subspecies of plant or animal, or an appreciable number of individuals of any one or more of these species; or

b) it is of special value for maintaining the genetic and ecological diversity of a region because of the quality and peculiarities of its flora and fauna; or

c) it is of special value as the habitat of plants or animals at a critical stage of their biological cycles; or

d) it is of special value for its endemic plant or animal species or communities.

3. Specific criteria for using waterfowl to identify wetlands of importance

A wetland should be considered internationally important if:

a) it regularly supports 20,000 waterfowl; or

b) it regularly supports substantial numbers of individuals from particular groups of waterfowl, indicative of wetland values, productivity or diversity; or

c) where data on populations are available, it regularly supports 1% of the individuals in a population of one species or subspecies of waterfowl.

In developing countries, a wetland could be considered for selection under Criterion 1 if, because of its outstanding hydrological, biological or ecological role, it is of substantial socio-economic and cultural value within the framework of sustainable use and habitat conservation.

Monitoring of Ramsar Sites

The maintenance of the ecological character of listed wetlands is perhaps the most important obligation accepted by Contracting Parties. There are, however, 46 Ramsar Sites which, according to the information available, have undergone, or are undergoing, or are likely to undergo a change in ecological character (RAMSAR, 1990b). When it comes to the attention of the Bureau that a Ramsar Site is likely to undergo a change in its ecological character, the Bureau, with the agreement of the Contracting Party, adds the site to the 'Montreux Record'. The Montreux Record is a register of Ramsar Sites where changes in ecological character have occurred, are occurring or are likely to occur.

Ramsar Sites in the Montreux Record have been the focus of the Ramsar Monitoring Procedure, which was established by the Standing Committee in 1988 as a formalised mechanism for the Bureau and the Contracting Parties to work together in assessing changes in the ecological character of listed wetlands. The Ramsar Monitoring Procedure has been applied to Lake Ichkeul in Tunisia (one of the first wetlands to be a subject of the Monitoring Procedure), Lake Nakuru in Kenya and the St Lucia Wetland System in South Africa. The Montreux Record is maintained as part of the Ramsar Database and is subject to continuous review. It indicates those sites where the Monitoring Procedure has been or is being implemented, as well as those sites where a Contracting Party has already identified remedial actions. Copies of the record are made available to Contracting Parties upon request to the Bureau and are included with the regular circulation of the Ramsar List to Contracting Parties.

Ramsar Wetland Conservation Fund

The Fourth Conference of the Contracting Parties to the Ramsar Convention (held at Montreux, Switzerland, 27 June to 4 July 1990) established a 'Wetland Conservation Fund' through its resolution C.4.3. This decision was an important recognition by the Contracting Parties that conservation and wise use of wetlands needs finance.

The fund essentially seeks to provide small grants for immediate action on defining sites, emergency action, promotional activities, or preparation of larger requests for submission to the development agencies. Requests can only be considered if they are supported by the government of an actual or a potential Contracting Party to the Ramsar Convention.

Operational guidelines of the Ramsar Wetland Conservation Fund specify five different types of activities which can receive an allocation from the Fund:

1. Preparatory assistance

Contracting Parties that are developing countries may request assistance for the purpose of preparing the designation of wetland sites for the Ramsar List of Wetlands of International Importance. Such assistance may include surveys, boundary delineation, evaluation of hydrological, biological and physical factors, identification of threats, preparation of national scientific inventories of wetlands suitable for designation, and help in designing requests to multilateral and bilateral assistance agencies for technical cooperation.

2. **Emergency assistance**

   Contracting parties that are developing countries may request emergency assistance for work in connection with wetland sites included in the List which have suffered change in ecological character or are in imminent danger of such change from technological developments, pollution, or other human interference. Such assistance may be available to draw up emergency measures for the safeguarding of the site.

3. **Training assistance**

   Contracting Parties that are developing countries may request emergency assistance for training of specialised staff for wetland conservation. Priority in training activities will be given to group training at local or regional levels, particularly at national or regional centres.

4. **Technical assistance**

   Contracting Parties that are developing countries may request assistance for wetland conservation projects for sites included in the List and for activities that will promote the wise use of wetlands in general.

5. **Assistance for promotional activities**

   The Fund may be used to support activities, including meetings, which could help to create interest in the Convention within countries of a given region, to create greater awareness of the issues related to the implementation of the Convention, or as a means of exchanging experiences and stimulating joint promotional activities. The fund may be used to support national activities for promoting the Convention when they concern meetings specifically organised to make the convention better known, for the creation of National Ramsar Committees, or the preparation of information materials for the general promotion of the Convention.

Kenya Wetlands Working Group

The Kenya Wetlands Working Group (KWWG) was set up to

"promote the conservation and wise use of wetland habitats in Kenya, according to the guidelines set out in the Ramsar Convention on Wetlands of International Importance ...".

The group arose from recommendations made at a workshop on 'Wetlands and Waterbirds in Eastern Africa' held in Uganda in March 1990, under the auspices of the International Waterfowl and Wetlands Research Bureau and the Institute of Environment and Natural Resources of Makerere University, Kampala. The Kenyan delegation to that workshop resolved to set up a national wetlands group and to become involved in the IWRB African Waterfowl Censuses. This was achieved by January 1991, when the Kenyan group carried out the first coordinated water-fowl census in association with 14 other African countries. Later in that year, the group expanded its interests to include wetland conservation and management for wise use and became the KWWG, a sub-group of the East Africa Natural History Society (Crafter *et al.*, 1992).

KWWG planned the Seminar on the Wetlands of Kenya (3-5 July, 1991) which was held in the National Museums of Kenya, Nairobi, with assistance from the IUCN Wetlands Programme and the IUCN Eastern Africa Regional Office. The gathering was attended by 130 people from 42 institutions, lasted three days and saw 20 papers presented and discussed.

KWWG is made up of representatives from the National Museums of Kenya, Kenya Wildlife Service, Society for Protection of the Environment in Kenya, East African Wildlife Society, East Africa Natural History Society, National Environment Secretariat, Kenyatta University and IUCN Eastern Africa Regional Office.

Bibliography

Crafter, S.A., S.G. Njuguna and G.W. Howard (Eds). 1992. *Wetlands of Kenya. Proceedings of the KWWG seminar on Wetlands of Kenya, National Museums of Kenya, Nairobi, Kenya 3-5 July 1991.* viii + 183 pp.

RAMSAR. 1990a. The Ramsar Convention: Convention on Wetlands of International Importance especially as Waterfowl Habitat. Ramsar Convention Bureau. 14 pp.

RAMSAR. 1990b. Convention on Wetlands of International Importance especially as Waterfowl Habitat. *Proceedings of the Fourth Meeting of the Conference of Contracting Parties, Montreux, Switzerland, 27 June to 4 July 1990.* Ramsar Convention Bureau. Vol. I. 306 pp.

RAMSAR. 1992. International Action for Wetlands. Project Submission to the Global Environment Facility. Ramsar Convention Bureau, Gland, Switzerland, March, 1992. 36 pp.

Discussions and Resolutions of the Seminar

Workshops

After the presentation of all papers, the participants divided into four groups which each reviewed and discussed a set of wetland topics to develop resolutions and recommendations. The following gives a brief description of the activities and findings of the four working groups.

Wetland planning, wetland management and the coordination of wetland activities

Chairperson: Mr G.K. Mango

The group investigated the institutional arrangements that might be required to develop a national wetlands programme, and how inter-departmental cooperation might be achieved. The group agreed that NEMC should be the coordinating authority for a wetlands conservation and management programme and that a number of committees should be established to ensure inter-departmental co-operation and collaboration.

Site projects for conservation and management of wise use of wetlands and the need for Environmental Impact Assessment for wetland developments

Chairperson: Prof. A. Kauzeni

The group reviewed those wetlands in Tanzania which are under threat and are in need of protection and it listed a number of critical sites. Several major sites were discussed as needing comprehensive conservation and management projects. The group also looked into existing policies and regulations regarding Environmental Impact Assessments (EIAs) and developed improved guidelines for development projects and proposals in wetlands

Priorities and organisations for research, inventories and monitoring

Chairperson: Prof. C.K. Omari

The group reviewed existing research arrangements and proposed that NEMC, together with the Institute of Resource Assessment and the Council of Science and Technology, should coordinate wetland research and create a library for wetland information. The group also proposed particular areas of research which are urgently required, such as studies on wetland dynamics, wetland processes and socio-economic values of wetlands. Finally the need for monitoring and regular assessments was stressed.

Wetland awareness and education and their roles in conservation

Chairperson: Mr J. Kabigumila

The group agreed that there is insufficient awareness of wetlands and no policy on wetland management. It was agreed that there is need for a wetlands awareness programme which should be directed at several target groups. These target groups were identified and activities were suggested. The group also proposed that a core group of wetland specialists should be established who would need to receive training in specific aspects of wetland management.

Resolutions and Recommendations of the Seminar

Below are the main resolutions of the seminar, as developed by the four workshops (above) and then discussed, modified and approved by the plenary seminar session. Details and supplementary notes for these resolutions follow as an Appendix. The order in which the resolutions appear is the same as that in the seminar and does not imply precedence or order of importance.

1. A National Wetlands Committee should be formed which would develop a National Wetlands Policy for Tanzania and Guidelines for the implementation of that Policy.

2. The National Wetlands Committee should be coordinated by the National Environment Management Council (NEMC) and should include representatives from all government bodies involved in wetland resource use, as well as representatives from other interested parties.

3. NEMC should convene a small Wetlands Steering Committee to develop the composition and mandate for the National Wetlands Committee and NEMC should solicit operating funds for wetlands activities (Appendix of Notes a).

4. The Wetlands Steering Committee should initiate the development of a National Wetlands Programme (to include the activities recommended here) within one year from the date of the meeting (Appendix of Notes b).

5. Tanzania should become a signatory to the Ramsar Convention on Wetlands of International Importance; NEMC should be the national authority to implement this and should form an expert group to select a wetland to be the first Ramsar site: e.g. Bahi Swamps, Lake Kitangiri, Wembere Swamps or Jozani Forest and wetlands.

6. There should be site projects for conservation and management for wise use of the following threatened wetlands of special importance (Appendix of Notes c):

    Bahi Swamps — Dodoma Region
    Lake Kitangiri — Singida Region
    Wembere Swamps — Tabora Region
    Malagarasi Swamps — Tabora/Kigoma Regions
    Water Falls — South Lake Tanganyika
    Jozani Forest and wetlands — Zanzibar
    Gombe Stream and Mahale Mountains — Kigoma Region
    Minziro Forest and coastal forests — Kagera Region

7. There should be site projects for conservation, management and wise multiple uses of the Kilombero Floodplain and the Rufiji Delta.

8. There should be EIAs and Statements for all development projects in wetlands (Appendix of Notes d).

9. There is need for an inventory of existing information on wetlands leading to a wetlands database which should be developed by NEMC, Institute of Resource Assessment and the Commission on Science and Technology; a national list of threatened wetlands should be established and there should be an inventory of wetland organisms.

10. Socio-economic studies on wetlands should be initiated and there should be documentation of the uses of wetlands by people in wetland areas - as well as studies of the dynamics and ecological processes in Tanzania's wetlands.

11. The impact of human activities on water catchments and associated wetlands should be appraised. There is a need for the examination of pollution of wetlands, including a study of suitable means of waste disposal.

12. Research and monitoring should begin on the problem of floating aquatic weeds.

13. Sufficient funds should be allocated for the resuscitation and maintenance of the hydrological monitoring system in wetlands and other water ways.

14. Wetland monitoring should be initiated to assess water quality and quantity, sedimentation and pollution, stocks of exploited species, important flora and fauna, human activities and impacts, etc. for the better management of wetland resources.

15. The concepts of wetland conservation and management should be incorporated into formal education programmes.

16. There should be a programme of public and government awareness of wetland issues (Appendix of Notes e).

17. There should be a training programme in wetland conservation and management for government officers and those involved in wetland issues.

Appendix of Notes

a. The Wetlands Steering Committee should comprise representatives from (at least) the Ministry of Agriculture, Tourism, Natural Resources and Environment; Ministry of Water, Energy and Minerals; Ministry of Industries and Trade; and Ministry of Local Government.

b. General guiding principles in the development of the National Wetlands Programme should be:

1   the integration of conservation and sustainable resource utilisation in the national interest;

2. the involvement of local resource users and wetland residents in the development of a National Wetlands Policy and at all stages of planning and implementation of specific projects in wetland areas.

c. Supporting information for site projects:

Bahi Swamps — migratory birds and fish fauna; threatened irrigation scheme

Lake Kitangiri — significant fishery, migratory birds, wildlife watering area; threatened rice scheme

Wembere Swamps — migratory bird refuge

Malagarasi Swamps — large wetland birds, important fishery, game controlled area, wildlife and hunting

Water Falls, Lake Tanganyika — little-known and unique area

Jozani Forest and wetlands — threatened rainforest and primates

Gombe Stream and Mahale Mountains — primates and other wildlife

Minziro and coastal forests — high levels of plant endemism

d. EIA recommendations:

1. before any project is undertaken in a wetland, an EIA must be carried out by national experts and then approved by the appropriate authority;

2. wetland projects that have been agreed upon or are in an advanced stage should be suspended until a thorough EIA has been completed; those that are about to start should be delayed until a quick EIA has been carried out;

3. NEMC should identify and prepare a list of experts who should conduct EIAs when required;

4. There is a need for legislation and regulation to incorporate EIAs in all wetland projects and EIA funding should be incorporated into project plans;

5. Relevant institutions should be informed about the plans for wetland projects at all stages of the planning process.

e. Target groups for wetlands awareness and education programmes should include:
    1. Wetland users and inhabitants - radio and meetings;
    2. Extension Officers - seminars, workshops, special training;
    3. Schools and colleges - curriculum, newsletters, Malaihai clubs;
    4. Politicians, policy makers and government officers - seminars and workshops;
    5. Media - seminars, workshops and press information.

Official closing of the Seminar on Wetlands of Tanzania

Mr A.D.O. Midelo
Municipal Director for Morogoro

It is indeed a privilege and great pleasure for me to officiate at the closing of the first seminar of its kind on the 'Wetlands of Tanzania'. On my own behalf and that of the Regional Administration, I extend a warm welcome to you all and hope you had a good stay in Morogoro.

This seminar gathered contributors from both within and outside Tanzania and included academics, researchers, environmentalists, ecologists, policy makers and experts on wetland conservation. I extend a further warm welcome to our brothers from Kenya, Uganda and Zambia who joined the endeavour to bring the wetlands issues to light. There was a wide coverage of a range of aspects concerning wetlands which included: overviews of Tanzania's wetlands; the various attributes of wetlands such as fishing, irrigation, ecological and socio-economic values; threats to the integrity of the wetland resource; and policies and issues governing the rational utilisation of wetlands. It is my conviction, therefore, that the exercise was not for academic purposes only, but also for the improvement of activities directed towards wetlands.

Your discussion dwelt on the status, utilisation and conservation of the nation's wetland endowment. I am convinced the contribution of wetlands to the socio-economic aspects of our people is enormous. Many questions need to be posed. Do we normally consider sustainable exploitation of these wetlands?

Do we consider the existence of other organisms and their interdependencies during planning? Do we really know that the depletion and degradation of wetlands can cause havoc to natural systems? These problems were tackled as well as many others. Your deliberations and recommendations focused on the following:

- the importance and values of wetlands;
- issues pertaining to the rational and sustainable utilisation of wetlands;
- the institutional framework and problems associated with its smooth functioning;
- the need for expanded public involvement, awareness and sensitisation;
- the importance of more research and information.

It is time we considered the values of our wetlands in planning processes at all levels. These processes should bear in mind the fragile and endemic nature of ecological systems. Consequently, implementation of environmental impact assessments should be conducted for projects that will impinge on wetlands.

There is quite a challenge before us all to make the public aware of their obligations towards wetlands. People should become involved at grassroot level so that their experiences and perceptions can be used in the planning and management processes. Raising of awareness should be accompanied by substantial scientific research and monitoring. It is my hope that these activities will be carried out simultaneously. All research findings should be made available to those who require them and I call upon you all, in particular the National Environmental Management Council, to create a wetland information system which will be accessible to everyone.

Sustainable development will depend on a sound natural resource base coupled with rational utilisation of resources of which wetlands are an integral part.

With these remarks, may I once again thank you very much for asking me to close this seminar. By this token I declare your seminar CLOSED.

Seminar attendance

Participants at the Seminar

Bakobi, B.L.M.	Principal Environment Education Officer, National Environment Management Council (NEMC), Ministry of Tourism, Natural Resources and Environment (MTNRE), P.O. Box 63154, Dar es Salaam
Bjarval, A.	Technical Advisor, NEMC, P.O. Box 63154, Dar es Salaam
Bwathondi, P.O.J.	Director-General, Tanzania Fisheries Research Institute, P.O. Box 9750, Dar es Salaam
Chooye, P.M.	Community Development Coordinator, WWF-Zambia Wetlands Project, NPWS, Private Bag 1, Chilanga, Zambia
Chimgege, T.	Forest Officer, Forestry and Beekeeping Division, MTNRE, P.O. Box 35066, Dar es Salaam
Faraji, S.	Senior Hydrologist, Water Research Division, Ministry of Water, Energy and Minerals, P.O. Box 35066, Dar es Salaam
Friederich, H.	Head of Project Management, IUCN Eastern Africa Regional Office, P.O. Box 68200, Nairobi, Kenya
Hojland, A.	Technical Advisor, NEMC, P.O. Box 63154, Dar es Salaam
Horrill, J.C.	Research Fellow, Institute of Marine Sciences, University of Dar es Salaam, P.O. Box 668, Zanzibar
Howard, G.W.	Regional Wetlands Coordinator, IUCN Eastern Africa Regional Office, P.O. Box 68200, Nairobi, Kenya
Hoza, R.B.	Fisheries Officer, Fisheries Division, MTNRE, P.O. Box 2462, Dar es Salaam
Juma, S.	Coordinator, Tanzania Environment Society, P.O. Box 1309, Dar es Salaam
Kabigumila, J.	Assistant Lecturer, Zoology Department, University of Dar es Salaam, P.O. Box 35065, Dar es Salaam
Kamukala, G.L.	Director-General, National Environment Management Council, P.O. Box 63154, Dar es Salaam
Kamuzora, G.	Assistant Director, Agriculture and Natural Resources Division, The Planning Commission, President's Office, P.O. Box 9242, Dar es Salaam
Kauzeni, A.	Professor, Institute of Resource Assessment, University of Dar es Salaam, P.O. Box 35097, Dar es Salaam
Kijumbe, E.J.	Announcer, Radio Tanzania, P.O. Box 9191, Dar es Salaam

Lamprey, R.	Ecologist, PAWM Project, Wildlife Division, P.O. Box 1994, Dar es Salaam
Luluhana, C.M.	General Manager, Dakawa Rice Farms Ltd., P.O. Box 972, Morogoro
Lweno, T.	Acting Director, Natural Resources Division, NEMC, P.O. Box 63154, Dar es Salaam
Mafabi, P.G.	Project Manager, National Wetlands Programme, P.O. Box 9629, Kampala, Uganda
Maganga, S.L.S.	Lecturer, Forest Biology Department, Sokoine University of Agriculture (SUA), P.O. Box 3008, Morogoro
Mango, G.K.	Acting Director, Physical Planning and Research Division, The Planning Commission, President's Office, P.O. Box 2420, Dar es Salaam
Manongi, F.	Instructor, College of African Wildlife Management, MWEKA, P.O. Box 3031, Moshi
Manongi, F.J.	Director of Planning, Rufiji Basin Development Authority, P.O. Box 9320, Dar es Salaam
Marwa, P.B.M.	Senior Industrial Engineer, Ministry of Industries and Trade, P.O. Box 9503, Dar es Salaam
Masija, E.H.	Assistant Commissioner, Irrigation, Ministry of Agriculture, Livestock Development and Co-operatives, P.O. Box 9192, Dar es Salaam
Maunya, M.	Journalist, *Daily News*, P.O. Box 9033, Dar es Salaam
Mayers, J.	Project Development Officer, WWF Country Office for Tanzania, P.O. Box 63117, Dar es Salaam
Mbonde, G.P.L.	Senior Forest Officer, Forestry and Beekeeping Division, MTNRE, P.O. Box 426, Dar es Salaam
Mihayo, J.M.	Senior Hydrologist, Ministry of Water, Energy and Minerals, P.O. Box 35066, Dar es Salaam
Miswala, S.K.	Catchment Officer, Forestry and Beekeeping Division, MTNRE, P.O. Box 1020, Morogoro
Mkuula S.	NEMC, P.O. Box 63154, Dar es Salaam
Mpemba, E.	Senior Game Management Officer, Wildlife Division, MTNRE, P.O. Box 1994, Dar es Salaam
Msaky, J.J.	Senior Lecturer, Department of Soil Science, SUA, P.O. Box 3008, Morogoro
Mugurusi, E.	Acting Director, Environment Division, MTNRE, P.O. Box 9372, Dar es Salaam
Mushobozi, C.N.	Senior Scientific Officer, Commission on Science and Technology, P.O. Box 4302, Dar es Salaam

Mwageni, E.A.	Assistant Lecturer, Faculty of Forestry, SUA, P.O. Box 3024, Morogoro
Mwalyosi, R.	Senior Research Fellow, Institute for Resource Assessment, University of Dar es Salaam, P.O. Box 35097, Dar es Salaam
Mwanukuzi, P.K.	Tutorial Assistant, Geography Department, University of Dar es Salaam, P.O. Box 35049, Dar es Salaam
Nasser, S.M.	Assistant Terrestrial Ecologist, Department of Environment, P.O. Box 811, Zanzibar
Ngaga, Y.M.	Assistant Lecturer, Forest Economics Department, SUA, P.O. Box 3008, Morogoro
Njuguna, S.	Associate Director, National Museums of Kenya, P.O. Box 40658, Nairobi, Kenya
Nnyiti, P.Y.	Conservation Officer, Wildlife Conservation Society of Tanzania, P.O. Box 70919, Dar es Salaam
Nshubemuki, L.	Forest Researcher, Tanzania Forestry Research Institute, P.O. Box 1854, Morogoro
Ogola, H.	Journalist, *Uhuru* and *Mzalendo,* P.O. Box 9221, Dar es Salaam
Omari, C.K.	Professor, Department of Sociology, University of Dar es Salaam, P.O. Box 35029, Dar es Salaam
Ruhinda, T.R.	Senior Scientific Officer, Commission for Science and Technology, P.O. Box 4302, Dar es Salaam
Saelie, G.A.	Economist, Ministry of Water, Energy and Minerals, P.O. Box 2000, Dar es Salaam
Tamatamah, R.A.	Fisheries Officer, Kunduchi Fisheries Institute, P.O. Box 60091, Dar es Salaam
Ubwani, Z.	Environmental Journalist, P.O. Box 70056, Dar es Salaam

Visitors to the Seminar

Dickinson, A.	Field Director, Society for Environmental Exploration, P.O. Box 2032, Dar es Salaam
Davies, S.	Conservationist, Royal Society for the Protection of Birds, The Lodge, Sandy Beds, England
Leach, K.R.	Environmental Geologist, Hardy BBT Africa Ltd., P.O. Box 963, Dar es Salaam
Midelo, A.D.O.	Municipal Director, Morogoro City Council
Murira, K.K.	Acting Director-General, Tanzania Forestry Research Institute, P.O. Box 1854, Morogoro
Tucker, G.	Dispersed Species Officer, International Council for Bird Preservation, 32 Cambridge Road, Girton, Cambridge, U.K.

The IUCN Wetlands Programme

Other titles in this series

Starting Mountaineering